ENKI BILAL

THE BEAST TRILOGY
CHAPTERS 1 & 2 - THE DORMANT BEAST/DECEMBER 32nd

Humanoids / DC Comics

ENKI BILAL, Writer/Artist
TARAS OTUS & SASHA WATSON, Translation

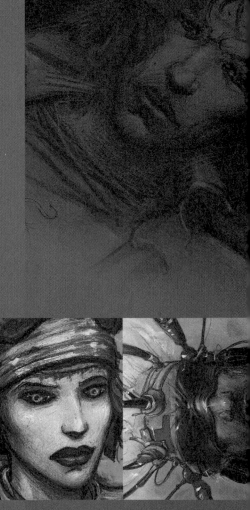

THIERRY FRISSEN, Book Design
STÉPHANE MARTINEZ & NATHALIE ROCHER, Letterers
PAUL BENJAMIN, Editor, Collected Edition
SHAWN M. GARRETT, Assistant Editor, Collected Edition
MAXIMILIEN CHAILLEUX & FABRICE GIGER, Editors, Original Edition

DC COMICS:
PAUL LEVITZ, President & Publisher
GEORG BREWER, VP-Design & Retail Product Development
RICHARD BRUNING, Senior VP-Creative Director
PATRICK CALDON, Senior VP-Finance & Operations
CHRIS CARAMALIS, VP-Finance
TERRI CUNNINGHAM, VP-Managing Editor
ALISON GILL, VP-Manufacturing
RICH JOHNSON, VP-Book Trade Sales
HANK KANALZ, VP-General Manager, WildStorm
LILLIAN LASERSON, Senior VP & General Counsel
JIM LEE, Editorial Director-WildStorm
DAVID MCKILLIPS, VP-Advertising & Custom Publishing
JOHN NEE, VP-Business Development
GREGORY NOVECK, Senior VP-Creative Affairs
CHERYL RUBIN, Senior VP-Brand Management
BOB WAYNE, VP-Sales & Marketing

THE BEAST TRILOGY: CHAPTER 1 & 2 - THE DORMANT BEAST/DECEMBER 32, Humanoids Publishing.
PO Box 931658, Hollywood, CA 90093. This is a publication of DC Comics, 1700 Broadway, New York,
NY 10019.

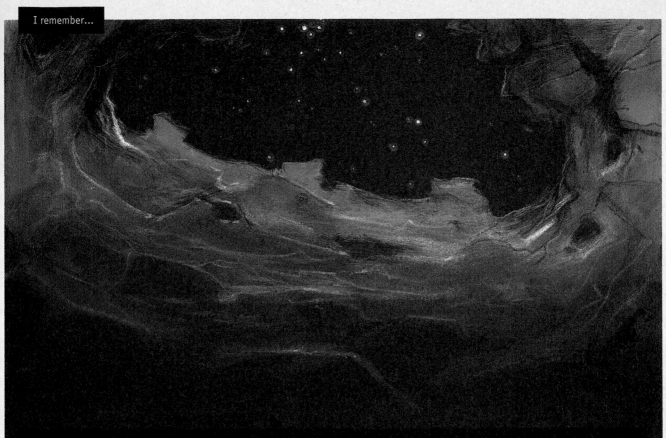

I remember...

I'm eighteen days old and I remember the huge black flies and the tepid summer air sinking in through the gaping holes in the hospital. Eighteen days old and I can already tell the difference between a blast of air and the blasting of bombs, between an exploding mortar and an exploding T34... Eighteen days old and I know that I'm an orphan and that my name is Nike... To my left, in the same bed, sleeps Amir, a day younger than I am, and to my right, Leyla, the youngest, barely ten days old, is crying... They too are orphans, but they don't know it. I'm the oldest and I swear by the stars that shine overhead, high above the roof that's been blown away, that I'll protect them forever. I swear it.

YOU CLAIM YOU CAN REALLY REMEMBER THAT? AT EIGHTEEN DAYS OLD?

YES.

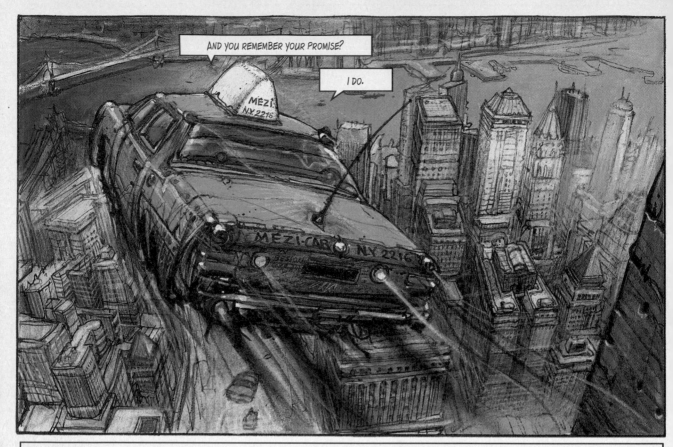

THEY SAY YOU WERE FOUND HOURS AFTER YOUR BIRTH, LYING NEXT TO A DEAD FIGHTER WEARING A BRAND OF SPORTS SHOES FROM THE LAST CENTURY: "NIKE"...
AND THAT'S HOW YOU GOT YOUR FIRST NAME...

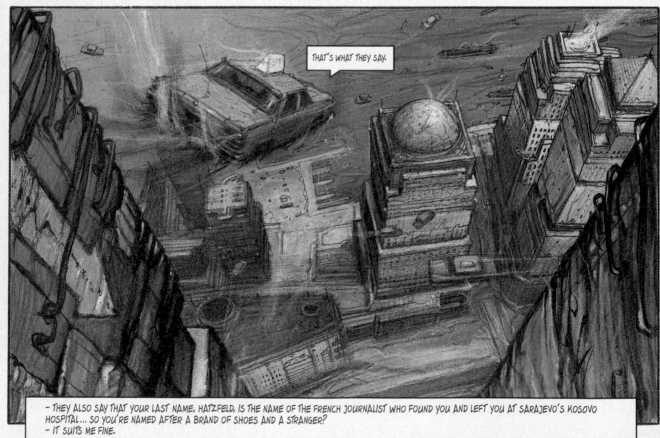

– THEY ALSO SAY THAT YOUR LAST NAME, HATZFELD, IS THE NAME OF THE FRENCH JOURNALIST WHO FOUND YOU AND LEFT YOU AT SARAJEVO'S KOSOVO HOSPITAL... SO YOU'RE NAMED AFTER A BRAND OF SHOES AND A STRANGER?
– IT SUITS ME FINE.

DO YOU THINK YOU CAN DIG DEEPLY ENOUGH IN YOUR MEMORY TO RETURN TO THESE EVENTS? PERHAPS EVEN TO DAY 1, THE DAY YOU WERE BORN?

I'M GETTING THERE... I'LL BE AT DAY 17 SOON...

WHAT ELSE CAN YOU TELL US ABOUT YOUR PHENOMENAL MEMORY?

...HAT IT'S ALLOWED ME TO MAKE LOTS OF MONEY, IVEN ME VIOLENT HEADACHES AND I CONTRIBUTED NORMOUSLY TO THE PROGRAMMING OF THE BWM.*

THEN WHY QUIT JUST WHEN THE BRAND NEW COMPUTER IS ABOUT TO BECOME OPERATIVE? DO YOU FEEL INFERIOR TO IT?

CBWM: CENTRAL BANK OF WORLD MEMORY (NYC-AMERICA).

- I SUPPOSE I WANT TO FIND AMIR AND LEYLA.
- THEY MAY BE DEAD NOW.
- NO.
- DID YOU GO TO SARAJEVO? DID YOU LOOK FOR THEM?
- THERE ARE NO RECORDS OF OUR BIRTH OVER THERE. THE HOSPITAL WAS DESTROYED ON DAY 27. THAT'S WHEN WE WERE SEPARATED. IT WAS IN AUGUST 1993. THIRTY-THREE YEARS, TWELVE DAYS, EIGHT HOURS AND SEVERAL MINUTES AGO.
- YET YOU SAY THAT YOU ARE A "MEMORY SPECIALIST WHO'S NOT INTERESTED IN THE PAST..."

...DON'T YOU THINK IT ALL SEEMS SOME-WHAT PARADOXICAL?

DROP ME OFF AT THE CORNER OF 22ND STREET, 3RD FLOOR. I HAVE A MEETING.

D17... I remember. The door of the hospital room opens violently. The smell I already know to be the smell of blood is so strong that I can taste it and it almost makes me throw up. Three orderlies speed by pushing a gurney, carrying a quivering pulp of red flesh. Someone says something about a shell exploding at a marketplace. I imagine my olfactory hypersensitivity dates back to this day.

AS ALWAYS AFTER A VIOLENT MEMORY FLASH, I NEED A BIG HIT OF OXYGEN TO BRING MY NEURONS BACK TO THE PRESENT. THE PRESENT MEANS A STRANGE MEETING WITH PAMELA WHICH I'D RATHER NOT ATTEND. IT'S BEEN THREE MONTHS SINCE OUR SUDDEN SEPARATION OR, SHOULD I SAY, HER DISAPPEARANCE. WHY DOES SHE WANT TO MEET AT THE THIRD FLOOR WATERSHOP?

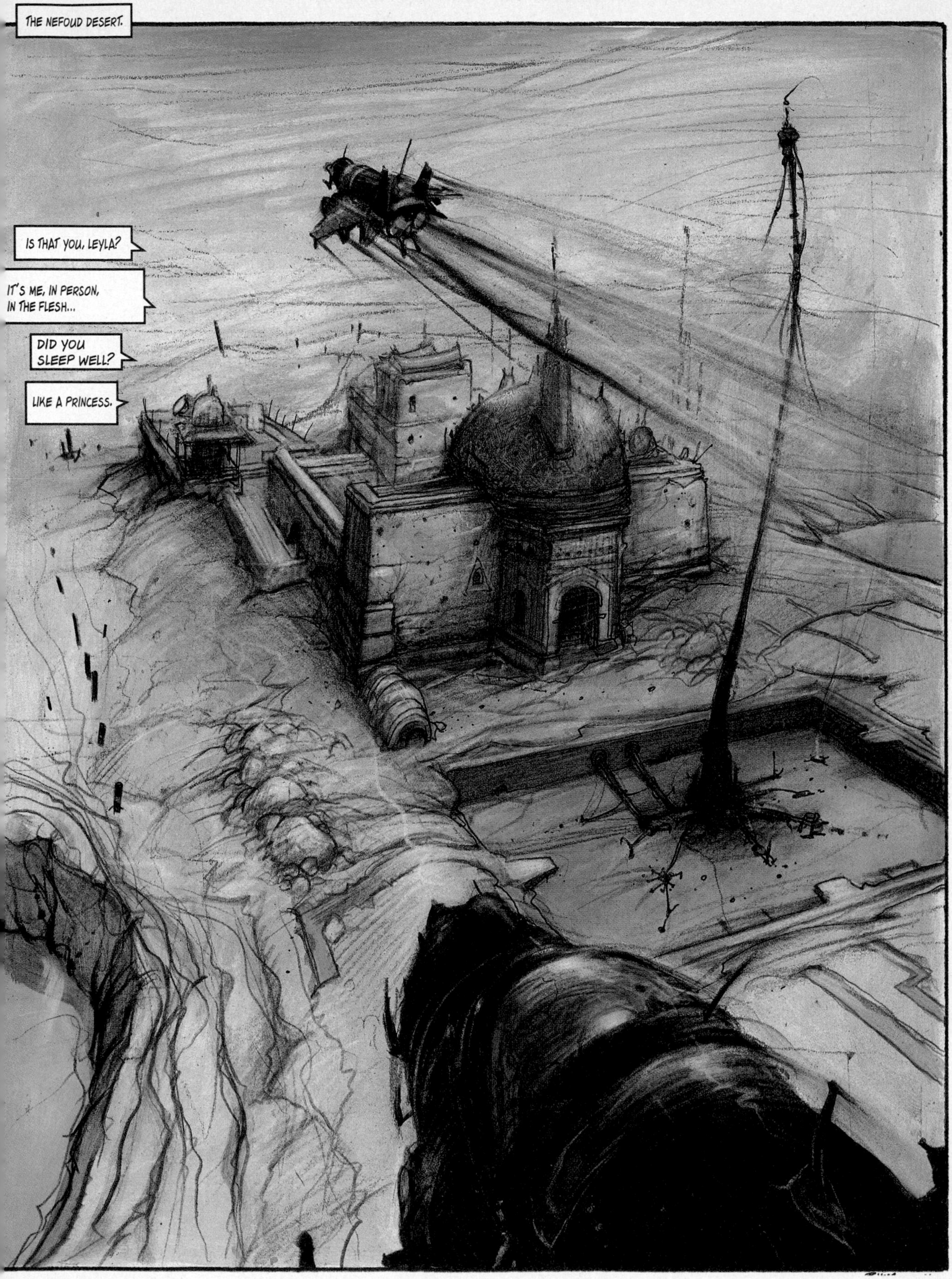
THE NEFOUD DESERT.
IS THAT YOU, LEYLA?
IT'S ME, IN PERSON, IN THE FLESH...
DID YOU SLEEP WELL?
LIKE A PRINCESS.

... AND THESE THINGS FLYING AROUND TODAY? YOUR PERSONAL GUARD?

YOU COULD SAY THAT.

FIGHTERS OR MISSILES?

FIGHTERS OF MISSILES.

THAT IS SOME-THING AND IT'S A VERY GOOD SIGN. YOU'LL BE ABLE TO SEE FAR SOON. VERY FAR.

I WANT TO ASK YOU A QUESTION, LEYLA.

AND YOU, DAD, HOW'RE YOUR EYES TODAY?

I CAN SEE AS FAR AS MY TOES, BUT THAT'S STILL SOMETHING, I SUPPOSE...

GO AHEAD.

WHAT'S GOING ON WITH YOUR ORBITING OBSERVATORY? YOU'RE HIDING SOMETHING FROM ME...

HUBBLE 4 IS FINE. IT SEES FAR. IT CAN SEE THE STARS ... AS YOU WILL SOON.

PRECISELY... WHAT DOES IT SEE? IS THERE A CONNECTION WITH ALL THE MILITARY ACTIVITY IN THE AREA? YOU TOLD ME YOU SPENT TWO WEEKS DIGGING IN THE DESERT. DID YOU FIND SOMETHING?

I CAN'T ANSWER YOU, DAD. AT LEAST NOT RIGHT NOW...

WILL YOU AT LEAST STAY A FEW DAYS?

NO, THEY'LL BE COMING FOR ME THIS EVENING. I'M GOING BACK TO THE HUBBLE. FINCH IS ALONE UP THERE AND I HAVE TO...

FINCH? YOU'RE STILL WITH FINCH?

AREN'T YOU GETTING A LITTLE NOSEY IN YOUR OLD AGE? SPEAKING OF WHICH, WHAT WOULD YOU LIKE FOR YOUR BIRTHDAY?

FOR MY 102ND BIRTHDAY, I'D LIKE YOU TO REACTIVATE "THE ELEVATOR TO THE STARS" ONE LAST TIME.

MANHATTAN WATER SHOP BUILDING.

PAMELA IS ALREADY THERE.

HER COLD BLANK EYES LOOK RIGHT THROUGH ME.

I REALLY DON'T LIKE BEING HERE. I WONDER WHY I KEEP WALKING TOWARDS HER INSTEAD OF TURNING AROUND AND RUNNING AWAY. I WONDER WHY SHE'S NOT ALONE.

HELLO, NIKE... I'D LIKE YOU TO MEET ION-ROBERT FUCK, A FRIEND.

PLEASED TO MEET YOU.

HER FRIEND WITH THE "FUCKED UP" NAME AND THE FAMILIAR "UPSIDE DOWN" SNARL OF A BENEZOPHRAINE USER IS TRULY UGLY.

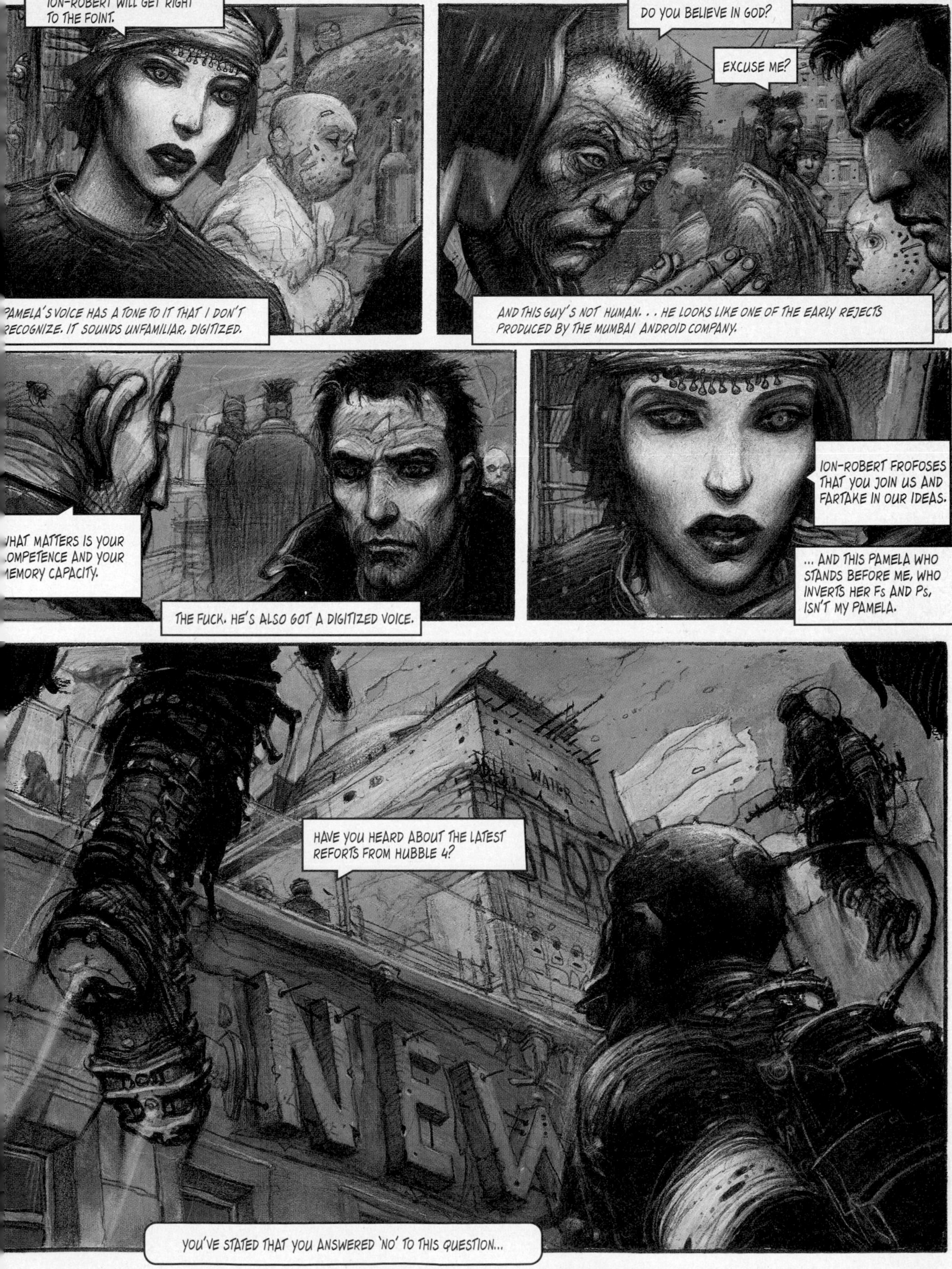
ION-ROBERT WILL GET RIGHT TO THE FOINT.
PAMELA'S VOICE HAS A TONE TO IT THAT I DON'T RECOGNIZE. IT SOUNDS UNFAMILIAR, DIGITIZED.
DO YOU BELIEVE IN GOD?
EXCUSE ME?
AND THIS GUY'S NOT HUMAN. . . HE LOOKS LIKE ONE OF THE EARLY REJECTS PRODUCED BY THE MUMBAI ANDROID COMPANY.
WHAT MATTERS IS YOUR COMPETENCE AND YOUR MEMORY CAPACITY.
THE FUCK. HE'S ALSO GOT A DIGITIZED VOICE.
ION-ROBERT FROFOSES THAT YOU JOIN US AND FARTAKE IN OUR IDEAS.
... AND THIS PAMELA WHO STANDS BEFORE ME, WHO INVERTS HER Fs AND Ps, ISN'T MY PAMELA.
HAVE YOU HEARD ABOUT THE LATEST REFORTS FROM HUBBLE 4?
YOU'VE STATED THAT YOU ANSWERED 'NO' TO THIS QUESTION...

" ... JUST BEFORE OUR 'KEIHILIN' UNIT ARRIVED AND SHOTS WERE FIRED."

YES. ONE ROUND DECAPITATED FUCK, I MEAN, PUCK... HIS HEAD SMASHED INTO MY FACE – I THOUGHT MY NOSE HAD EXPLODED.

"ANOTHER ROUND CUT PAMELA'S BODY IN HALF I DIDN'T KNOW WHAT WAS GOING ON. I WAS LEAKING BLOOD AND THERE WAS PAMELA IN TWO PIECES... THE FAKE PAMELA, THAT IS."

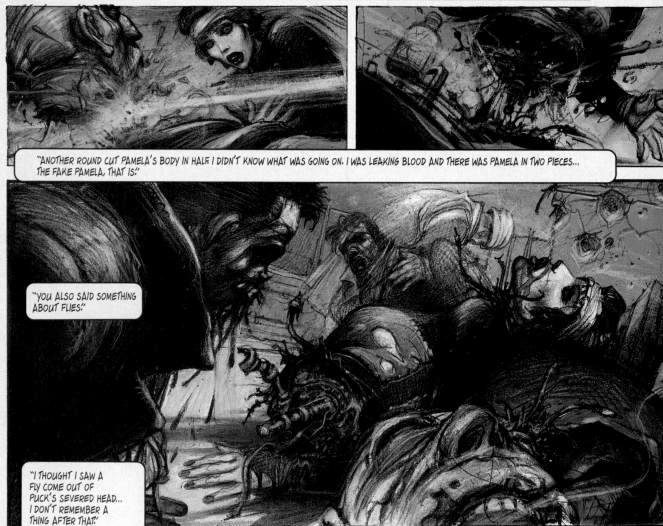

"YOU ALSO SAID SOMETHING ABOUT FLIES."

"I THOUGHT I SAW A FLY COME OUT OF PUCK'S SEVERED HEAD... I DON'T REMEMBER A THING AFTER THAT."

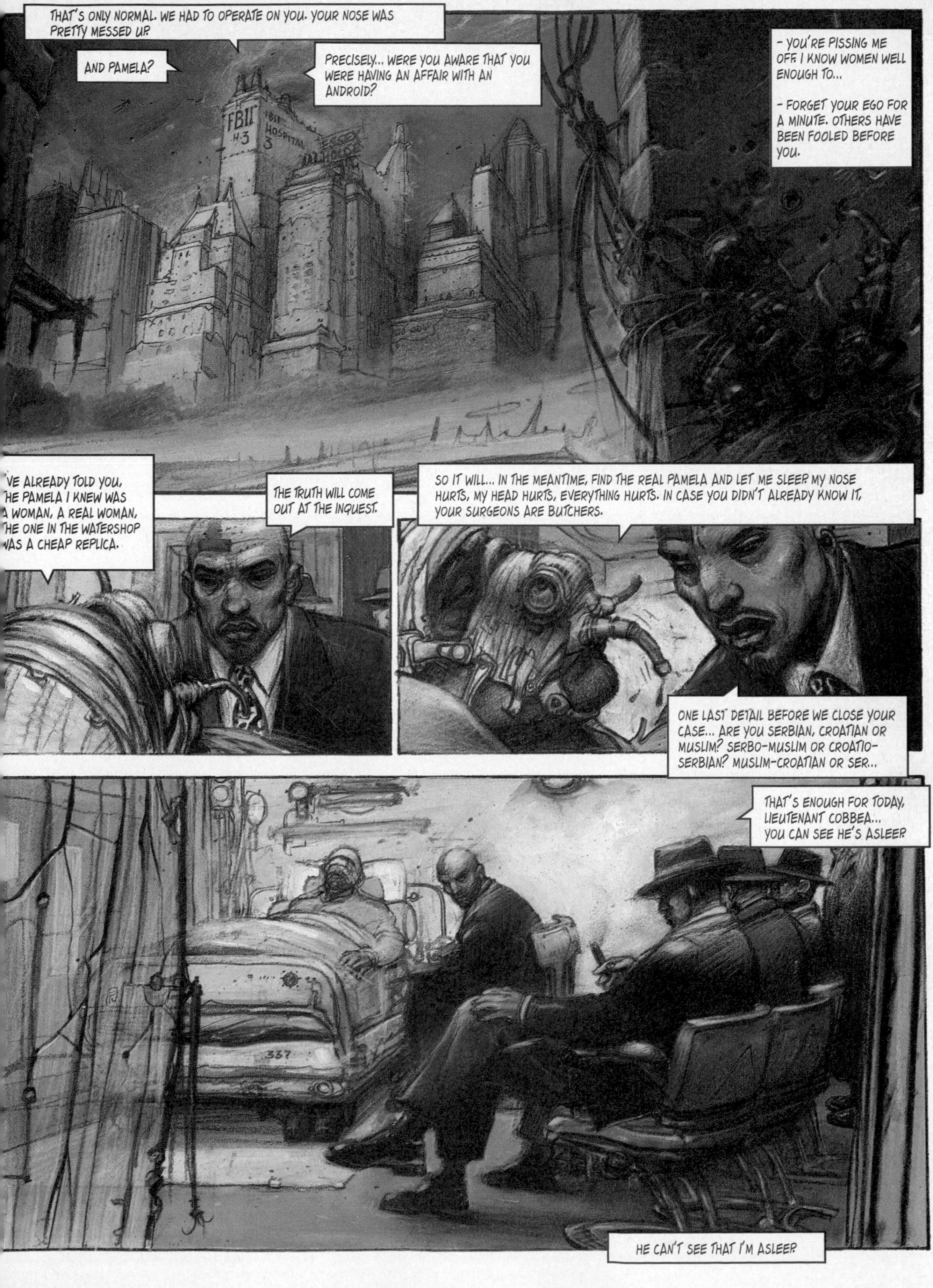
THAT'S ONLY NORMAL. WE HAD TO OPERATE ON YOU. YOUR NOSE WAS PRETTY MESSED UP.
AND PAMELA?
PRECISELY... WERE YOU AWARE THAT YOU WERE HAVING AN AFFAIR WITH AN ANDROID?
- YOU'RE PISSING ME OFF. I KNOW WOMEN WELL ENOUGH TO...
- FORGET YOUR EGO FOR A MINUTE. OTHERS HAVE BEEN FOOLED BEFORE YOU.
FBII H-3
FBII HOSPITAL 3
'VE ALREADY TOLD YOU, THE PAMELA I KNEW WAS A WOMAN, A REAL WOMAN, THE ONE IN THE WATERSHOP WAS A CHEAP REPLICA.
THE TRUTH WILL COME OUT AT THE INQUEST.
SO IT WILL... IN THE MEANTIME, FIND THE REAL PAMELA AND LET ME SLEEP. MY NOSE HURTS, MY HEAD HURTS, EVERYTHING HURTS. IN CASE YOU DIDN'T ALREADY KNOW IT, YOUR SURGEONS ARE BUTCHERS.
ONE LAST DETAIL BEFORE WE CLOSE YOUR CASE... ARE YOU SERBIAN, CROATIAN OR MUSLIM? SERBO-MUSLIM OR CROATIO-SERBIAN? MUSLIM-CROATIAN OR SER...
THAT'S ENOUGH FOR TODAY, LIEUTENANT COBBEA... YOU CAN SEE HE'S ASLEEP.
337
HE CAN'T SEE THAT I'M ASLEEP.

D.16... Warhole - the hole the war has left in the ceiling above my always wide-open eyes. I am 16 days old and I understand English... A cripple passing by swears in Serbo-Croatian: "Jebem ti rat i rupu!" it means, "Fuck the war and the hole."

MOSCOW-AIR QUALITY: COLD (-22°C) POISONOUS TO VERY POISONOUS (7/10).

14

OKAY!

SURPRISE NUMBER ONE! DON'T TURN AROUND AND KEEP YOUR EYES CLOSED.

HERE.

HEY!!!!

WHAT IS THIS DISGUSTING THING?

IMPORTED WILD TUNA, FRESHLY DEFROSTED TO BE EATEN RAW AS SASHIMI.

YOU DON'T KNOW WHAT'S GOOD...

IT STINKS!

D15... I remember that I need a change of diapers. I'm stewing in piss and shit and have been for hours. Where are the nurses? I can hear them talk about a visit from some French intellectuals. I just want them to change my diapers. I start bawling louder than I ever have before in my short 15-day life. Amir joins in. We want to be clean.

NEXT SURPRISE... YOU CAN TURN AROUND NOW.

SHIT. A "KEIHILIN" OUTF WHERE'D YOU GET THAT

IT'S A GIFT FROM OUR NEW EMPLOYERS... THERE'S ONE FOR YOU, TOO... YOU CAN FLY WITH ONE OF THESE... THE FBII USES THE SAME ONES...

DID YOU LAND A CONTRACT?

ALMOST... THEY'RE COMING TO GET US IN A FEW DAYS. IF WE PASS THEIR TESTS, THEY'LL HIRE US AND PAY OUR RENT FOR A YEAR.

WHAT WOULD WE HAVE TO DO?

STAKEOUTS OR SOME- THING.

YOU KNOW I'D KISS YOU, SACHA, IF ONLY I COULD...

ACTUALLY, YOU CAN.

OW IT'S YOUR TURN TO CLOSE YOUR EYES.

ONLY ON ONE CONDITION, MY LITTLE AMIR.

YOU GET TO CARVE THE STINKY TUNA.

SO I'M DEAD.

SO YOU'RE DEAD.

ESSEX HOUSE

WWW123X//AC 95002CCXCC WWW123X//AC 95002CXCC

ND
adway Publications

Associate Directors: Sébastien Gnaedig & Didier Gonord

NEW YORKER-DAILY

== MANHATTAN ==

ATTACK AT THE WATERSHOP
NIKE HATZFELD DEAD

We have learned from official sources that Nike Hatzfeld, the specialist in memory investigation, has died as a result of wounds received at the Watershop shooting which invol-opposing factions of the Mafia. Based on th-was confirmed that th-

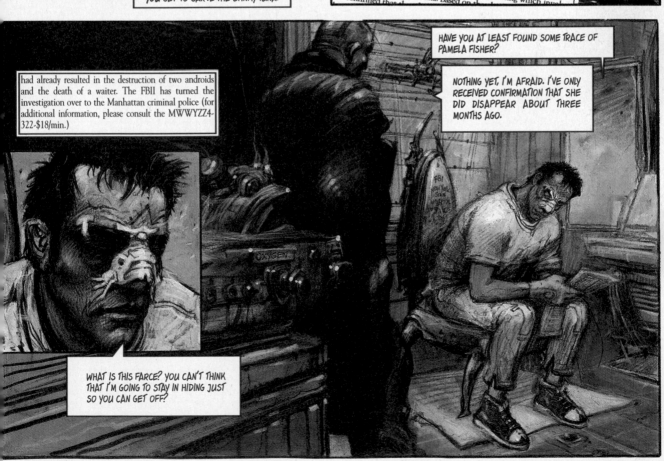

had already resulted in the destruction of two androids and the death of a waiter. The FBII has turned the investigation over to the Manhattan criminal police (for additional information, please consult the MWWYZZ4-322-$18/min.)

HAVE YOU AT LEAST FOUND SOME TRACE OF PAMELA FISHER?

NOTHING YET, I'M AFRAID. I'VE ONLY RECEIVED CONFIRMATION THAT SHE DID DISAPPEAR ABOUT THREE MONTHS AGO.

WHAT IS THIS FARCE? YOU CAN'T THINK THAT I'M GOING TO STAY IN HIDING JUST SO YOU CAN GET OFF?

I SUPPOSE YOU'VE HEARD OF THE *OBSCURANTIS ORDER*, THE DOUBLE O?

THE LITTLE FUNDAMENTALIST MAFIA?

THEY'RE GROWING AND EXPANDING IN ALL DIRECTIONS. THEY'RE A REAL MILITARY THREAT.

DON'T BE SO REDUCTIVE. THE LITTLE FUNDAMENTALIST MAFIA IS IN THE MIDST OF A GREAT MUTATION.

WHAT HAS THIS GOT TO DO WITH ME?

LET ME EXPLAIN...

– I'M SURE YOU KNOW THAT THE NUMBER ONE MEMBERS OF THE OBSCURANTIS ORDER – THAT IS HOW THEY REFER TO THEIR THREE NEW, CHARISMATIC AND SELF-PROCLAIMED LEADERS – HAVE DECIDED TO ACCELERATE THE DEATH OF EVERYTHING THAT HAS TO DO WITH THOUGHT, SCIENCE, CULTURE AND MEMORY... YOU'RE ON A LIST OF SOME TEN THOUSAND PEOPLE ON EARTH WHO INTEREST THEM.
THE LIST IS DIVIDED INTO TWO CATEGORIES: THOSE THEY WILL ELIMINATE AND THOSE THEY WILL INSTRUMENTALIZE. IT IS MY PLEASURE TO INFORM YOU THAT THEY APPARENTLY PUT YOU IN THE SECOND CATEGORY.
THE BIONIC PAMELA WAS PART OF THE FIRST PHASE OF YOUR INSTRUMENTALIZATION.

– SO...

WELL, I JUST RECEIVED HER AUTOPSY REPORT. SHE WAS STUFFED WITH FAIRLY SOPHISTICATED MICRO-SCANNERS.

– IF YOU'D SPENT A SINGLE NIGHT IN THE ARMS OF THAT CREATURE, YOU'D HAVE BEEN DIGITALIZED DOWN TO THE SMALLEST DETAILS, YOUR EVERY MENTAL OR PHYSICAL FEATURE. FOR YOUR SAKE, I HOPE YOU MANAGED TO STEER CLEAR.

– I TOLD YOU I ONLY SLEPT WITH THE REAL PAMELA...
HOW'S THE INVESTIGATION GOING?

– THE AUTHORITIES ON PARASITOLOGY AND THE MOLECULAR BIOLOGY OF THE PREDATORY DIPTERA HAVE PLACED PAMELA FISHER IN THE CATEGORY OF "POTENTIAL INSTRUMENTALIZABLES"
... I'VE PUT OUT AN INTERNATIONAL SEARCH WARRANT, THOUGH I DON'T HAVE MUCH HOPE OF FINDING HER...

THE SLIGHTEST SPECK OF HER SKIN, EVEN HER MUCUS, COULD DIGITALLY MEMORIZE EVERYTHING THE FIVE HUMAN SENSES CAN PERCEIVE.

ONE THING IS CLEAR... IF THEY "CALLED" YOU FOR THIS MEETING AT THE WATERSHOP, IT WAS BECAUSE THEY'D DECIDED TO "SUBDUE" YOU. WE FOUND A NUMBER OF INTERESTING SUBSTANCES UNDER THE PAMELA FISHER REPLICA'S NAILS...

HOW DID YOU KNOW ABOUT THE RENDEZVOUS? WAS IT THE NEW YORK JOURNALIST?

... THERE WAS ENOUGH THERE TO MAKE YOU FOLLOW HER TO THE ENDS OF THE EARTH LIKE A DOCILE PUPPY.

EXACTLY...SHE'S ONE OF OUR BEST AGENTS.

- SHE'S BEEN "FOLLOWING" YOU FOR QUITE SOME TIME, LIKE MANY OF THE CBWM SPECIALISTS ... SHE'D COME TO BELIEVE THAT THE DOUBLE O WAS INTERESTED IN YOUR MEMORY CAPABILITIES IN RELATION TO THEIR INFAMOUS PLAN FOR HISTORICAL REVISIONISM. COUNTLESS HISTORIANS, NOVELISTS AND SCREENWRITERS AROUND THE WORLD HAVE ALREADY BEEN INSTRUMENTALIZED BY THE OBSCURANTIS ORDER.

- I'VE HEARD ABOUT THIS PLAN. IT'S INSANE, I DON'T BELIEVE IT.

- YOU'RE WRONG, NIKE, WE'RE AT WAR! YOU'VE NO IDEA HOW FAR IT'S GONE.

- AND YOU, LIEUTENANT COBBEA, HAVE YOU GOT ANY IDEA WHAT A HEADACHE IS? AND A NOSE... A NOSE THAT'S BEEN SHREDDED AND THEN REBUILT WITHOUT CARE? DO YOU KNOW? CAN YOU REMEMBER?

- ?

AND CAN YOU HEAR THE SHOT FIRED IN "SNIPER ALLEY?"

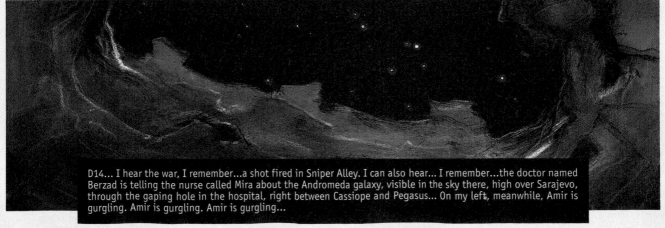

D14... I hear the war, I remember...a shot fired in Sniper Alley. I can also hear... I remember...the doctor named Berzad is telling the nurse called Mira about the Andromeda galaxy, visible in the sky there, high over Sarajevo, through the gaping hole in the hospital, right between Cassiope and Pegasus... On my left, meanwhile, Amir is gurgling. Amir is gurgling. Amir is gurgling...

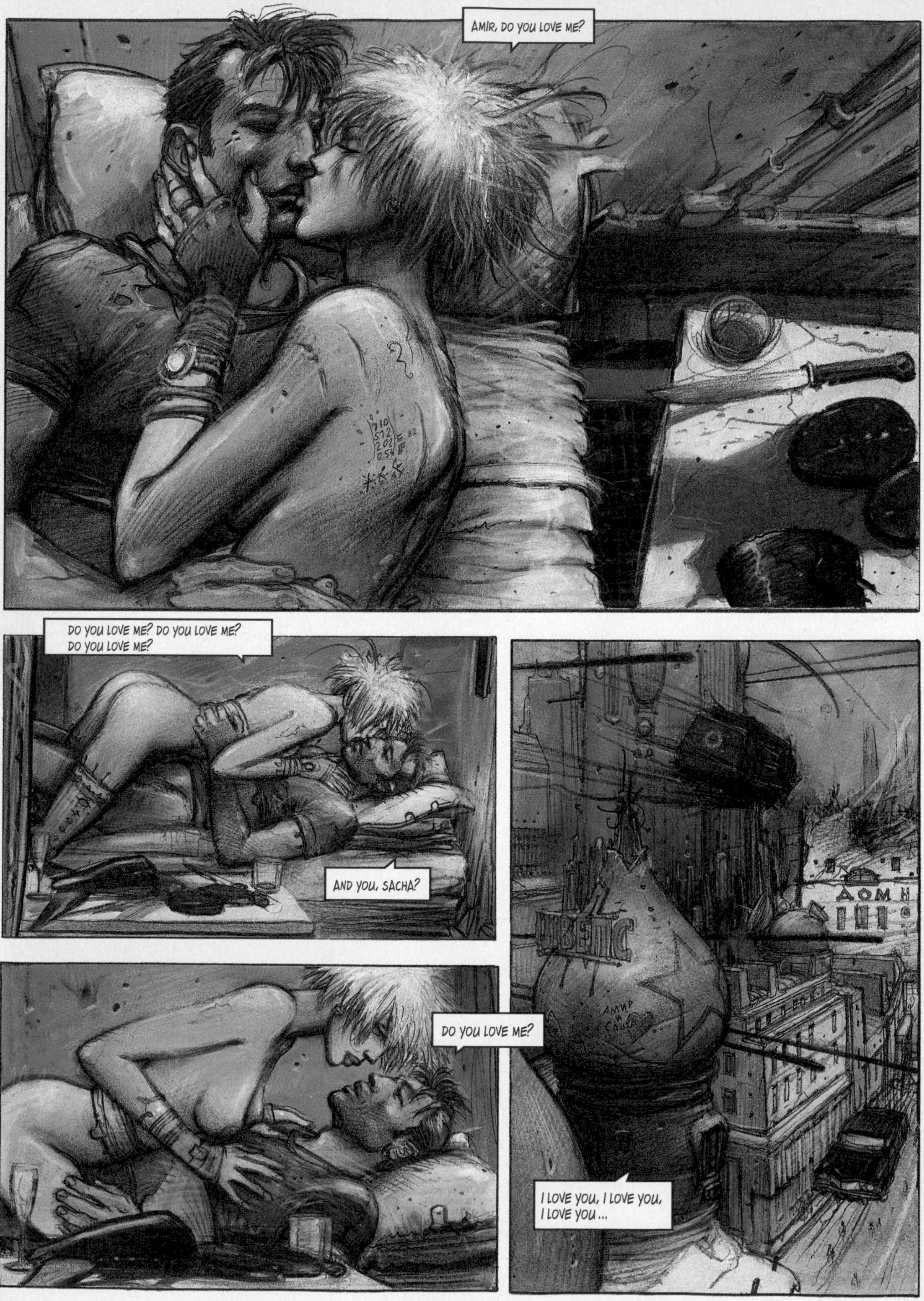
AMIR, DO YOU LOVE ME?
DO YOU LOVE ME? DO YOU LOVE ME? DO YOU LOVE ME?
AND YOU, SACHA?
DO YOU LOVE ME?
I LOVE YOU, I LOVE YOU, I LOVE YOU ...

THE KARA SEA.

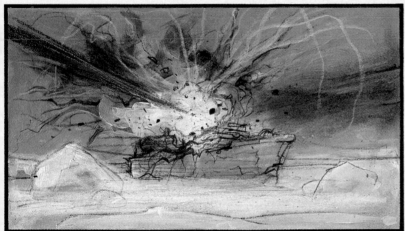

WE KNOW THAT THE "T. BRAHE," ONE OF THE VERY LAST SPACE SURVEILLANCE SHIPS STILL IN SERVICE, HAD 74 CREW MEMBERS AND 27 ASTROPHYSICISTS ON BOARD. ALTHOUGH NO ONE HAS CLAIMED RESPONSIBILITY FOR THIS MOST RECENT ATTACK, IT SEEMS TO BEAR THE SIGNATURE OF THE MOST EXTREME FACTION OF THE OBSCURANTIS ORDER. THE DISCOMFORT OF AUTHORITIES, BOTH SECTARIAN AND ALSO RELIGIOUS MODERATES CLOSE TO THE OBSCURANTISTS, SEEMS TO CONFIRM THIS HYPOTHESIS. ON ANOTHER FRONT, THE EXTREMIST FACTION'S ACCESS TO HIGHLY SOPHISTICATED WEAPONRY ADDS TO MOUNTING CONCERNS AT NATO AND THE UNITED NATIONS. THERE ARE PARTICULAR FEARS THAT THE LASER WEAPONS FOR SATELLITES AND BOMBERS, LEFT BEHIND BY THE MAFIA NETWORKS OF THE FORMER SOVIET UNION, MAY HAVE ALREADY FALLEN INTO THE HANDS OF..

ACHA, ARE YOU SURE THAT UR FUTURE EMPLOYERS AREN'T VOLVED IN THIS SHIT?

JUST READ THE CONTRACTS.

COME ON, OPEN YOUR MOUTH INSTEAD OF TALKING NONSENSE.

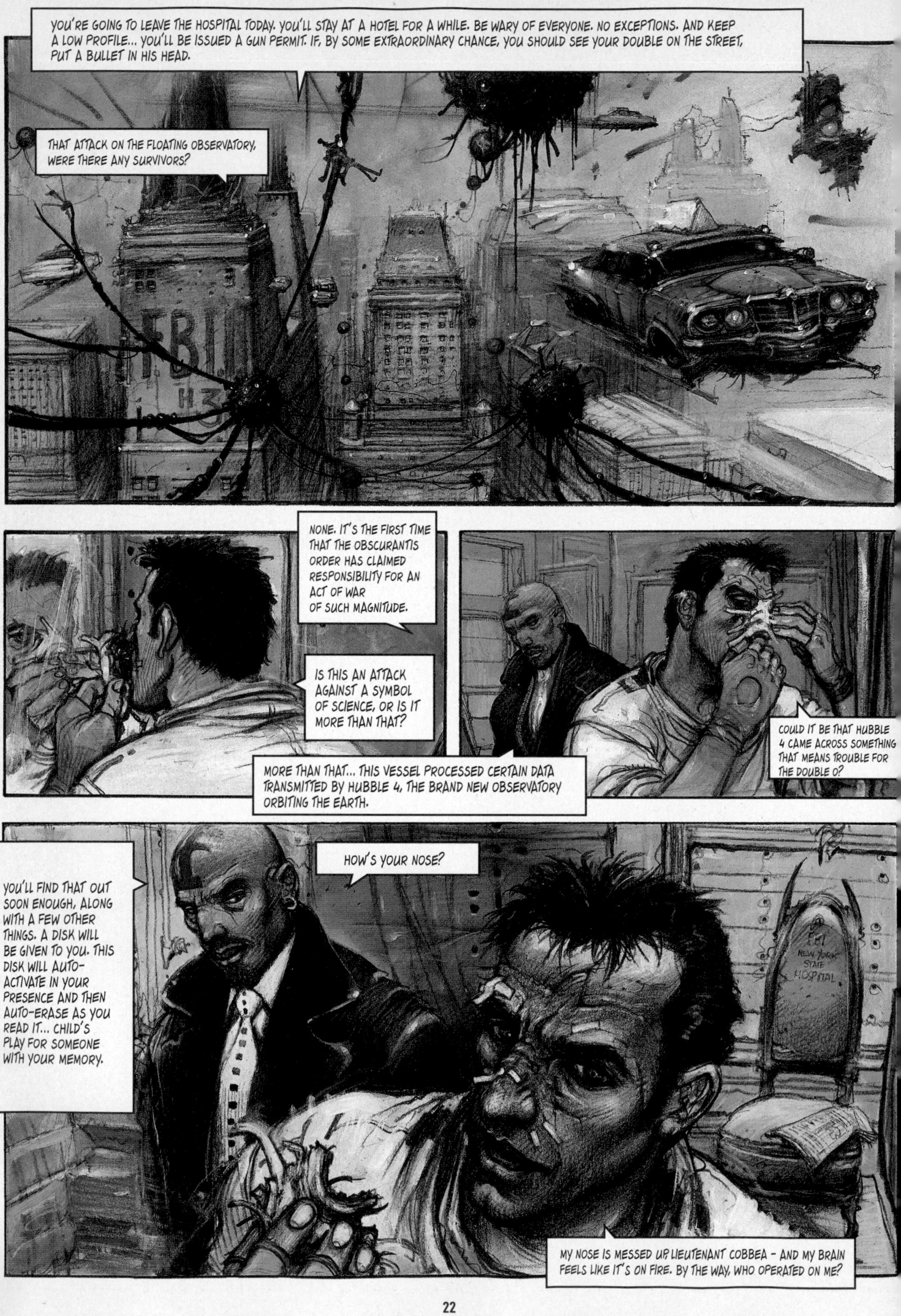
YOU'RE GOING TO LEAVE THE HOSPITAL TODAY. YOU'LL STAY AT A HOTEL FOR A WHILE. BE WARY OF EVERYONE. NO EXCEPTIONS. AND KEEP A LOW PROFILE... YOU'LL BE ISSUED A GUN PERMIT. IF, BY SOME EXTRAORDINARY CHANCE, YOU SHOULD SEE YOUR DOUBLE ON THE STREET, PUT A BULLET IN HIS HEAD.
THAT ATTACK ON THE FLOATING OBSERVATORY, WERE THERE ANY SURVIVORS?
NONE. IT'S THE FIRST TIME THAT THE OBSCURANTIS ORDER HAS CLAIMED RESPONSIBILITY FOR AN ACT OF WAR OF SUCH MAGNITUDE.
IS THIS AN ATTACK AGAINST A SYMBOL OF SCIENCE, OR IS IT MORE THAN THAT?
MORE THAN THAT... THIS VESSEL PROCESSED CERTAIN DATA TRANSMITTED BY HUBBLE 4, THE BRAND NEW OBSERVATORY ORBITING THE EARTH.
COULD IT BE THAT HUBBLE 4 CAME ACROSS SOMETHING THAT MEANS TROUBLE FOR THE DOUBLE O?
YOU'LL FIND THAT OUT SOON ENOUGH, ALONG WITH A FEW OTHER THINGS. A DISK WILL BE GIVEN TO YOU. THIS DISK WILL AUTO-ACTIVATE IN YOUR PRESENCE AND THEN AUTO-ERASE AS YOU READ IT... CHILD'S PLAY FOR SOMEONE WITH YOUR MEMORY.
HOW'S YOUR NOSE?
MY NOSE IS MESSED UP, LIEUTENANT COBBEA - AND MY BRAIN FEELS LIKE IT'S ON FIRE. BY THE WAY, WHO OPERATED ON ME?

THREE DAYS — AND SEVENTY-TWO HOURS OF PAIN — LATER, ESSEX HOUSE HOTEL (SINGLE ROOM).

WHO OPERATED ON ME?

CONSULTATIONS WITH THE DOCTORS ARE FOR FBII MEMBERS ONLY. BESIDES, ACCORDING TO OUR FILES, YOU'RE DECEASED. "NIKE HATZFELD — DECEASED." I REPEAT, "DECEASED." WHAT'S MORE, I SEE HERE THAT YOU'RE "REPLICABLE." HOW DO I KNOW THAT YOU'RE THE ORIGINAL NIKE HATZFELD?

LET ME SPEAK TO LIEUTENANT COBBEA.

WE CAN'T GIVE OUT THAT KIND OF INFORMATION — IT'S A MILITARY SECRET.

FUCK YOU AND YOUR MILITARY SECRETS! I'VE HAD A BURNING PAIN IN MY FRONTAL LOBE EVER SINCE YOUR FUCKING OPERATION. MY HEAD'S GOING TO EXPLODE. I DEMAND TO SEE A DOCTOR.

LIEUTENANT COBBEA HAS BEEN TRANSFERRED. AS FOR YOUR MIGRAINES, WHOEVER YOU ARE, TAKE SOME ASPIRALGAN, THREE TABLETS, THREE TIMES A DAY, IT'S OVER THE COUNTER. GOOD LUCK.

FUCK YOU!!!

THAT SAME NIGHT I RECEIVE AN EXXA-21 PISTOL (GLOVES INCLUDED) WITH A DISK IN THE EPHEMERAL DRIVE AND, EVEN BETTER, A BOTTLE OF SAINT-ESTEPHE HAUT-MARBUZET 1999 (FRENCH), WHICH IS VERY, VERY EXPENSIVE. ALL OF IT SENT BY THE TRANSFERRED (I DON'T BELIEVE IT FOR ONE SECOND) COBBEA.

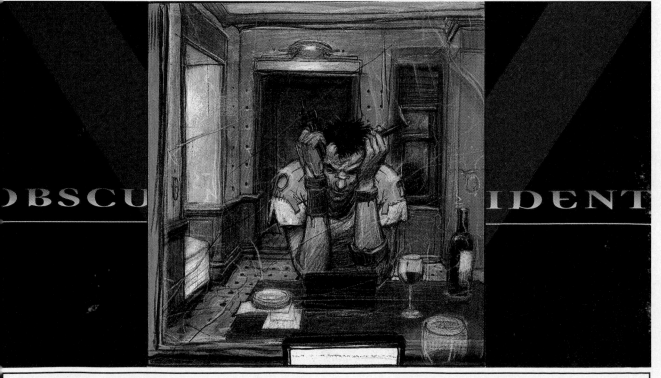

THE DISK AUTO-ACTIVATES LATE THAT NIGHT, THE BOTTLE OF SAINT-ESTEPHE HAS BEEN EMPTY FOR QUITE SOME TIME AND THE WORDS, AS PROMISED, AUTO-ERASE AS I READ THEM.

Confidential document U.N. Security Dept.
Minimum Information: Keys Required for Thesaurus.

OBSCURANTIS ORDER
(Generic Markers - development and information press +XXW1133-O.R.)

Preamble *Mafiosi infection within early 21st century Neo-Conservatism. Serious nuclear disasters (2003-2004, in Ukraine, Russia, Siberia, Pakistan), a legacy of the last century's ill-managed post-Soviet era. Rise of neo-sects and of barbaric, religious neo-fundamentalism.*

Summary. *Genesis 2017* Creation of the Radical Monotheistic Movement OBSCURANTIS ORDER, by a dissident group of fundamentalists emerging from the three principal monotheistic sectors (Judaism, Christianity, Islam) with the support of the African Mafias and occult financial groups. Three major action areas are designated: THOUGHT, SCIENCE, CULTURE.
Objectives: INTERNATIONAL OBSCURANTIS and a widespread planetary TABULA RASA.

CONFIDENTIAL OBSCURANTIS ORDER

Summary. *Development - 2018-2022* - The "Great Auto-da-fé" is ordered. The Tribe of the "Eradicators" is formed. Pakistani "neo-Talibanism" spreads to Africa and to Mediterranean Europe (subcontracting, "Vatican dissident"). Beginning of the Tabula Rasa policy. Systematic destruction of cultural and scientific assets in all religious protectorates controlled by the Obscurantis Order. Implantation of powerful proselytizing networks in neo-conservative Europe and in the United States. Publication on parchment of the first precepts of the Double O, in the famous Dictionary of the same name. Language is purified and only 499 words are permissible and taught. Creation of the first internment camps by the "ERADICATORS."

2022-2025 Assassination Attempts

The signing by the legal theocracies (under the aegis of the New United Nations) of the "Treaty of Tehran," condemning the Obscurantis Orderin its "entirety."

Random suicide attacks.

**THE SELF-PROCLAIMED
HARD-EDGED EXTREMIST FACTION** (MINORITY)
*This faction is linked to the hypothetical existence of extra-
terrestrial life (a radio signal emanating from the Eagle nebula.)*

February 2026 - FIRST RADIO SIGNAL emanating from the EAGLE NEBULA (M16) Hubble 4
sighting of deep transformations in the "EGC" (evaporation globules of gases) of the nebula's great
pillar. Hubble receives the "FIRST SIGNAL" from a mutant "EGC" directed at Earth. The destination
point is kept secret: LOCKED INFORMATION.
Code Name Eagle Site. The armed forces of the New United Nations take over the case. Civilians
privy to this secret can be counted on one hand (astrophysicists and scientists only).
April 2026 - SECOND and THIRD SIGNAL. SAME DESTINATION POINT.

CONFIDENTIAL OBSCURANTIS ORDER

This discovery and its potential implications
(extra-terrestrial life ? - raising doubt
regarding the existence of a single Deity)
are unacceptable to the Obscurantis Order.
Self-Proclamation of the Number One
dissidents (3?) - and murderous radicalization.
Destruction of the mythic Observatory of
Mount Palomar Station and of the floating
T. Brahe Observatory. Desperate attempts at
locating the Eagle Site.

EAGLE SITE: LOCKED INFORMATION

THE BATTLE AGAINST THE OBSCURANTIS ORDER
- Military activities on a global scale and attempts at locating
and destroying the Eradicators' camps.
LOCKED INFORMATION.
- Coordinated investigations by the Secret Service organizations
of 98 countries. The search for the Number Ones of the Double O.
- The Warhole Plan with the support of the F.B.I.I. (Federal Bureau
of International Investigation.) (Bio of Dr. Warhole locked.)

Cobbea to Mister Nike.
Regarding you and the fake Pamela...
I fear that you did sleep with her...
As to the "real" one, it would seem that
she'd been a student of Warhole's.
Beware of Warhole!
It's possible that War-

SEVERAL DAYS LATER. THE NEFOUD DESERT.

I DON'T SEE ANYTHING, LEYLA. IT'S BLURRY AND DARK.

DARKNESS CAN'T BE BLURRY, DADDY. YOU HAVE TO FOCUS THE LEFT EYE AT INFINITY.

THERE IT IS... I SEE SOMETHING... I SEE ANDROMEDA.

RAISE YOUR HEAD VERTICALLY A LITTLE AND ZOOM OUT.

THE ONLY BRIGHT SPOT YOU'LL SEE MOVING IS ME, THE HUBBLE

I GOT IT, LEYLA, I CAN SEE YOU, I CAN EVEN SEE YOUR EYES.

AREN'T YOU EXAGGERATING A LITTLE?

I CAN EVEN SEE THAT MISCHIEVOUS LOOK IN YOUR EYES. WHAT ARE YOU UP TO?

AM I MISTAKEN OR IS IT GOING TO BE YOUR BIRTHDAY SOON?

LEYLA, CAN YOU HEAR ME? CUT YOUR COM LINE AND COME SEE. I'M IN MODULE 3.

26

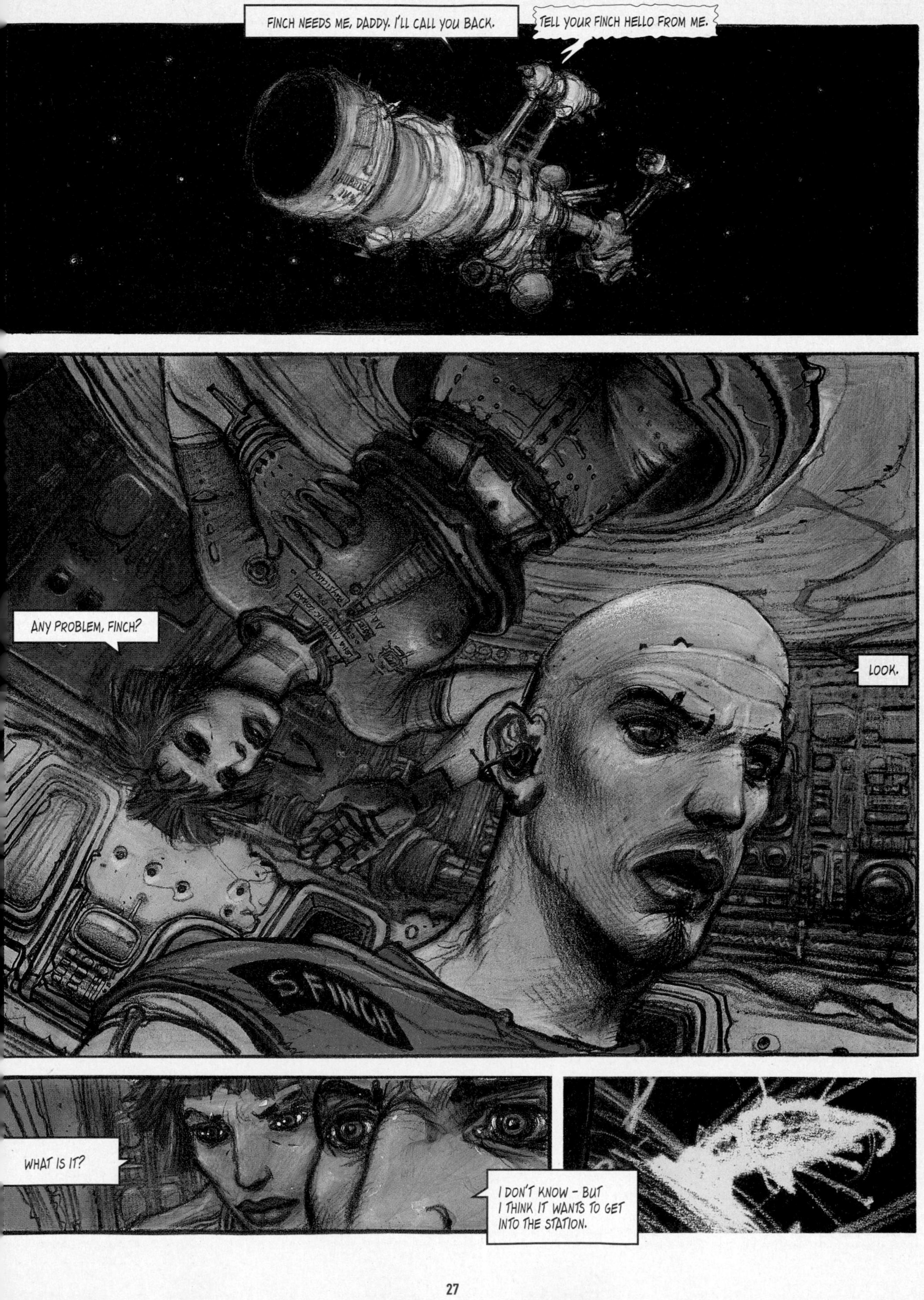
FINCH NEEDS ME, DADDY. I'LL CALL YOU BACK.
TELL YOUR FINCH HELLO FROM ME.
ANY PROBLEM, FINCH?
LOOK.
S. FINCH
WHAT IS IT?
I DON'T KNOW - BUT I THINK IT WANTS TO GET INTO THE STATION.

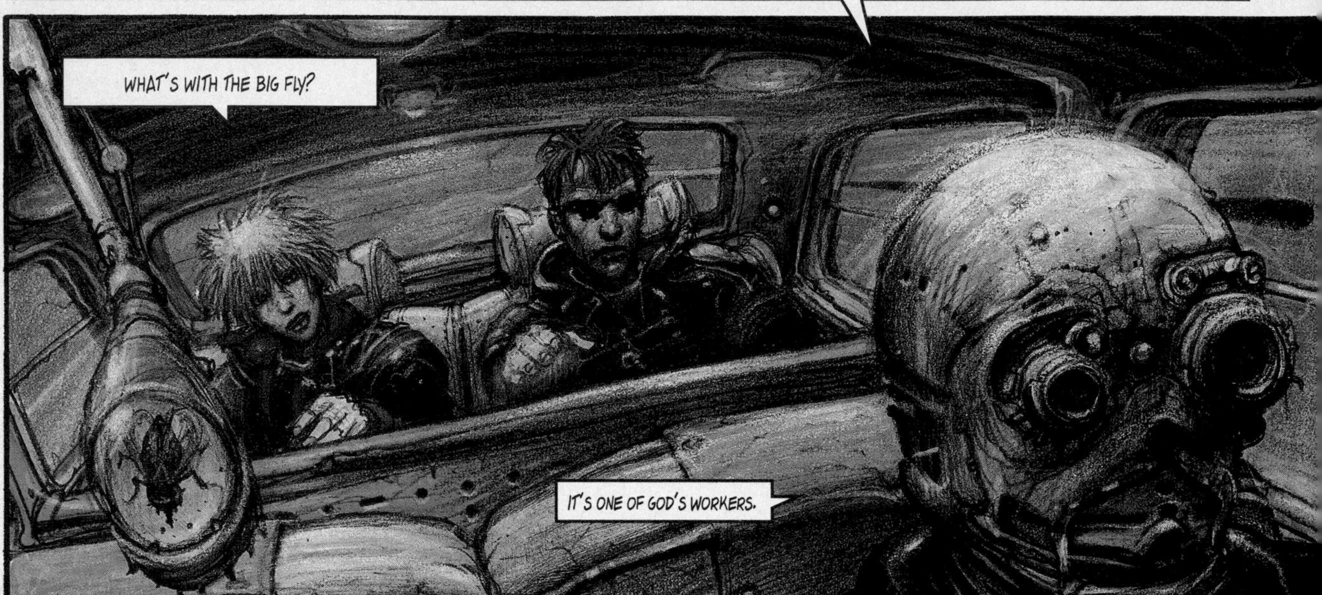
I'M PLEASED TO NOTE THAT YOU'RE WEARING YOUR K SUITS. I HOPE THEY'LL BRING YOU SATISFACTION. MORE IMPORTANTLY, I HOPE THAT THEY'LL REINFORCE THE THREE Fs: FORCE, FIDELITY AND FAITH.
WHAT'S WITH THE BIG FLY?
IT'S ONE OF GOD'S WORKERS.

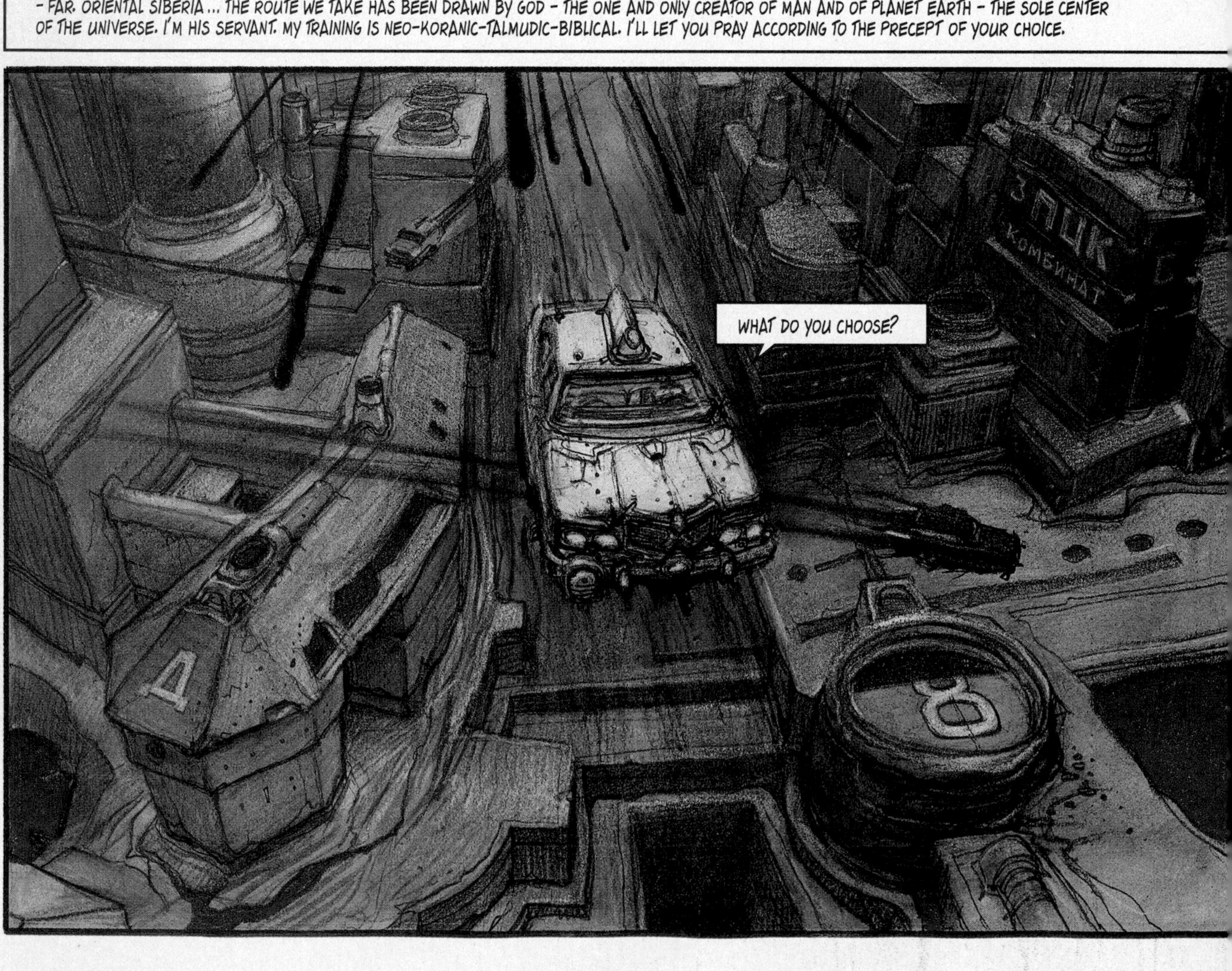
- I SEE... AND CAN YOU TELL US WHERE WE'RE GOING?
- FAR. ORIENTAL SIBERIA... THE ROUTE WE TAKE HAS BEEN DRAWN BY GOD - THE ONE AND ONLY CREATOR OF MAN AND OF PLANET EARTH - THE SOLE CENTER OF THE UNIVERSE. I'M HIS SERVANT. MY TRAINING IS NEO-KORANIC-TALMUDIC-BIBLICAL. I'LL LET YOU PRAY ACCORDING TO THE PRECEPT OF YOUR CHOICE.
WHAT DO YOU CHOOSE?

I HATE TO DISAPPOINT YOU, BUT MY GIRLFRIEND AND I AREN'T REALLY BELIEVERS.

THAT IS DISTRESSING. RELIGIOUS PRACTICE IS HIGHLY ADVISABLE IN THIS VEHICLE.

WHAT ABOUT SEXUAL PRACTICE? WHAT WOULD YOU SAY IF WE WANTED TO MAKE LOVELY LOVE?

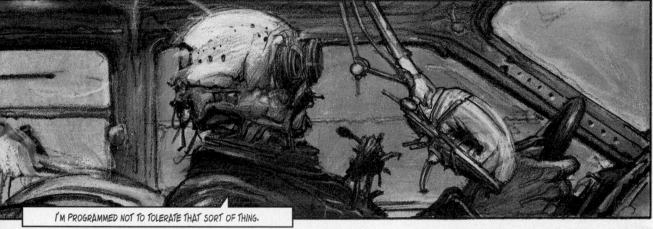

I'M PROGRAMMED NOT TO TOLERATE THAT SORT OF THING.

BESIDES, YOU MUST KNOW PERFECTLY WELL THAT ERADICATORS DON'T FORNICATE.

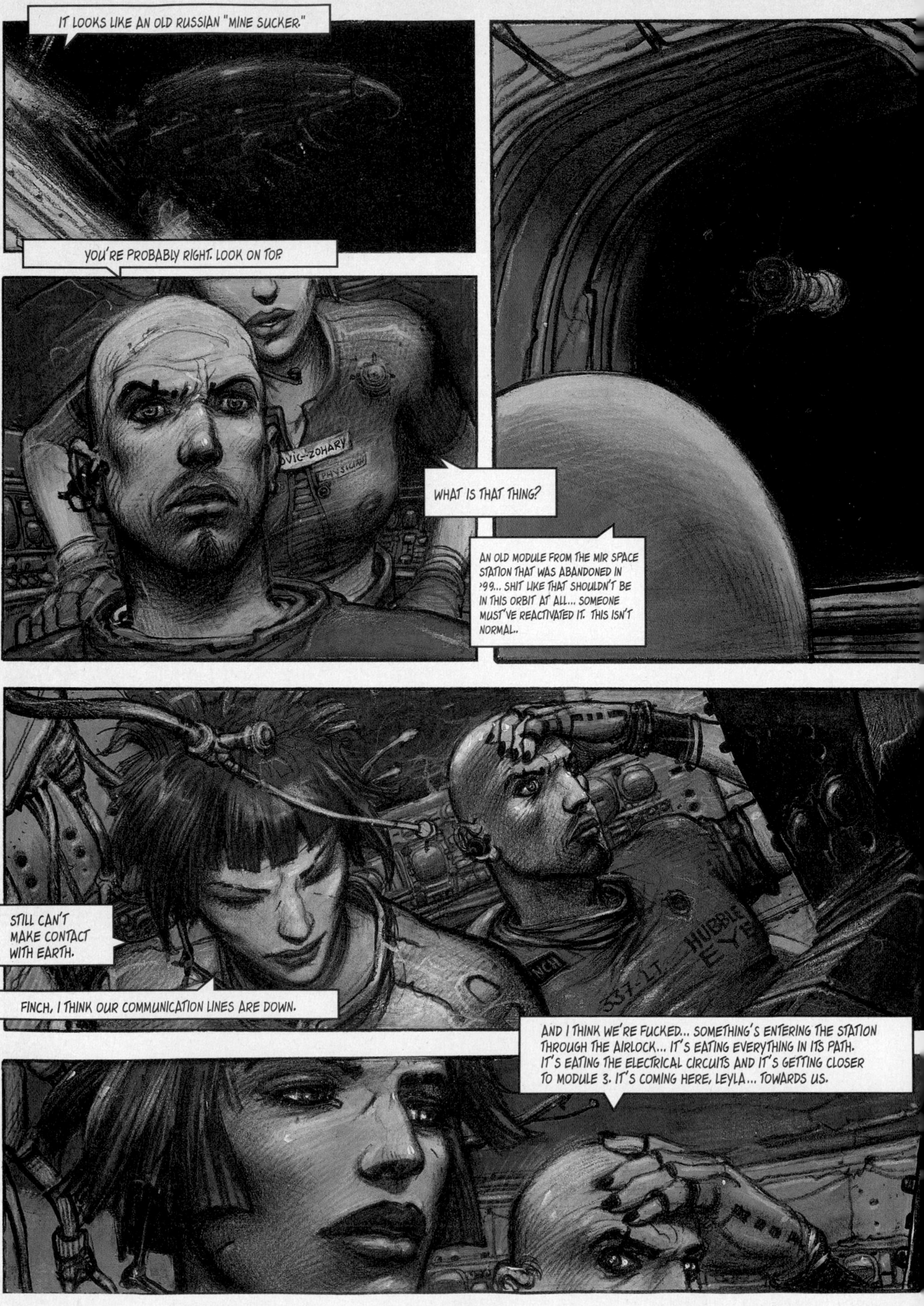
IT LOOKS LIKE AN OLD RUSSIAN "MINE SUCKER."
YOU'RE PROBABLY RIGHT. LOOK ON TOP.
WHAT IS THAT THING?
AN OLD MODULE FROM THE MIR SPACE STATION THAT WAS ABANDONED IN '99... SHIT LIKE THAT SHOULDN'T BE IN THIS ORBIT AT ALL... SOMEONE MUST'VE REACTIVATED IT. THIS ISN'T NORMAL..
STILL CAN'T MAKE CONTACT WITH EARTH.
FINCH, I THINK OUR COMMUNICATION LINES ARE DOWN.
AND I THINK WE'RE FUCKED... SOMETHING'S ENTERING THE STATION THROUGH THE AIRLOCK... IT'S EATING EVERYTHING IN ITS PATH. IT'S EATING THE ELECTRICAL CIRCUITS AND IT'S GETTING CLOSER TO MODULE 3. IT'S COMING HERE, LEYLA... TOWARDS US.

SWALLOWING A DOZEN ASPIRALGAN TABLETS DOES NOTHING. LET IT BE KNOWN THAT PAIN STILL INHABITS MY SKULL WITH GREAT DEDICATION AND INSOLENCE. IT IS PRECISE, INCANDESCENT AND IMMOVABLE.

I THINK MY RECKLESS TRIP EAST OF CHINATOWN LEVEL 4 TO "LITTLE BANGKOK" WAS A FINAL GAMBLE BEFORE MY HEAD EXPLODES.

I HADN'T SEEN OLD KOETSU FOR YEARS, EVER SINCE HIS CONVICTION AND MULTIPLE PRISON SEN-TENCES.

HIS CONSULTATIONS ARE ALWAYS ILLEGAL AND RIDICULOUSLY EXPENSIVE. BUT HIS SCIENCE IS INTACT... THAT, AT LEAST, IS WHAT I PSYCH MYSELF INTO BELIEVING.

FUCKIN' KOETSU, YOU'D BETTER MAKE THIS PAIN GO AWAY.

HE'S SET UP HIS TRANSIENT PRACTICE AT THE VERY TOP OF SOME UNFINISHED SKYSCRAPERS, WHERE THE MAFIA NETWORKS WEAVE AND UNWEAVE LIKE THE STARS; IT'S BOTH VIRTUAL AND CLANDESTINE, HERE ONE DAY, GONE THE NEXT... TODAY IT'S RIGHT THERE!

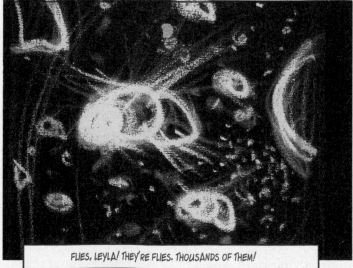

FLIES, LEYLA! THEY'RE FLIES. THOUSANDS OF THEM!

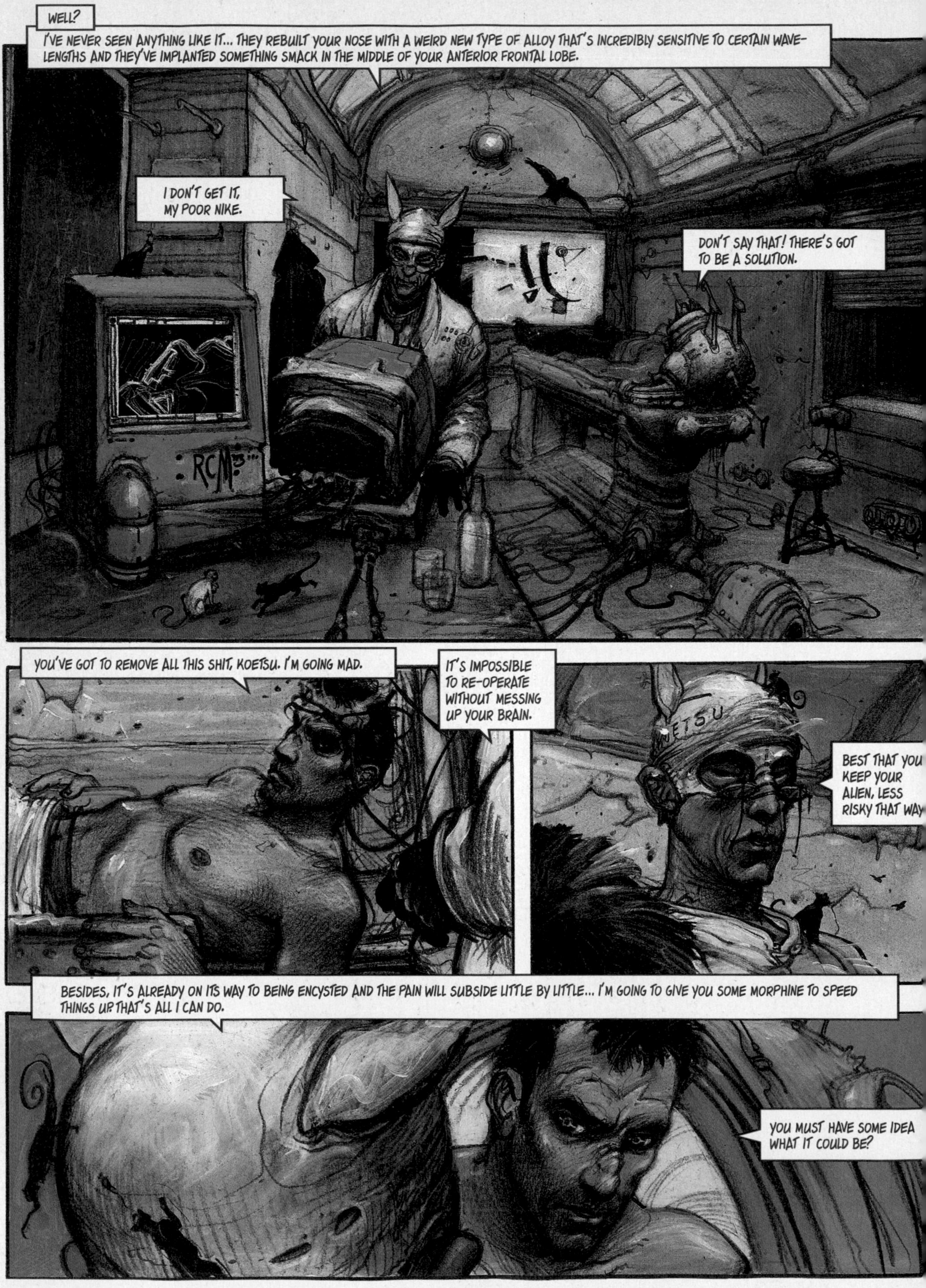
WELL?
I'VE NEVER SEEN ANYTHING LIKE IT... THEY REBUILT YOUR NOSE WITH A WEIRD NEW TYPE OF ALLOY THAT'S INCREDIBLY SENSITIVE TO CERTAIN WAVE-LENGTHS AND THEY'VE IMPLANTED SOMETHING SMACK IN THE MIDDLE OF YOUR ANTERIOR FRONTAL LOBE.
I DON'T GET IT, MY POOR NIKE.
DON'T SAY THAT! THERE'S GOT TO BE A SOLUTION.
RCM
YOU'VE GOT TO REMOVE ALL THIS SHIT, KOETSU. I'M GOING MAD.
IT'S IMPOSSIBLE TO RE-OPERATE WITHOUT MESSING UP YOUR BRAIN.
BEST THAT YOU KEEP YOUR ALIEN, LESS RISKY THAT WAY
BESIDES, IT'S ALREADY ON ITS WAY TO BEING ENCYSTED AND THE PAIN WILL SUBSIDE LITTLE BY LITTLE... I'M GOING TO GIVE YOU SOME MORPHINE TO SPEED THINGS UP. THAT'S ALL I CAN DO.
YOU MUST HAVE SOME IDEA WHAT IT COULD BE?

OR MAYBE YOU KNOW AND DON'T WANT TO TELL ME.

I REALLY DON'T KNOW, NIKE... IT LOOKS LIKE A MICRO-TRANSMITTER, OR A RECEIVER... OR SOMETHING LIKE THAT.

OR MAYBE IT'S JUST SOMETHING THE SURGEON FORGOT, THAT HAPPENS... YOU'RE GONNA HAVE TO DEAL WITH THE MESS YOU'RE IN ON YOUR OWN... ME, I DON'T WANT TO KNOW ANYTHING. NOT HOW OR WHY IT GOT INTO YOUR BRAIN. I'VE GOT ENOUGH SHIT TO DEAL WITH ALREADY.

I'M GOING TO GIVE YOU A SHOT OF TRIPLE-GRADUATED-DELAYED-ACTION SUPERMORPHINE.

'M ALSO GIVING YOU AN ANALGESIC HELMET TO WEAR FOR 24 OURS... IT'S LIGHT. THAT SHOULD HELP

IT'S MORE THAN THE SURPRISINGLY HEAVY HELMET THAT COMES TO ME. D.13, A BLOOD RED HELMET, IN SARAJEVO 1993.

D.13... Night at the hospital. A man sobs in the corridor. Amir and Leyla listen with their foreheads abnormally creased up. I sense the brightness of their eyes and their little bodies wound into taut question marks. What is this terrible sound, more terrible than the cry of the wounded, more terrifying than the silence of the dead?

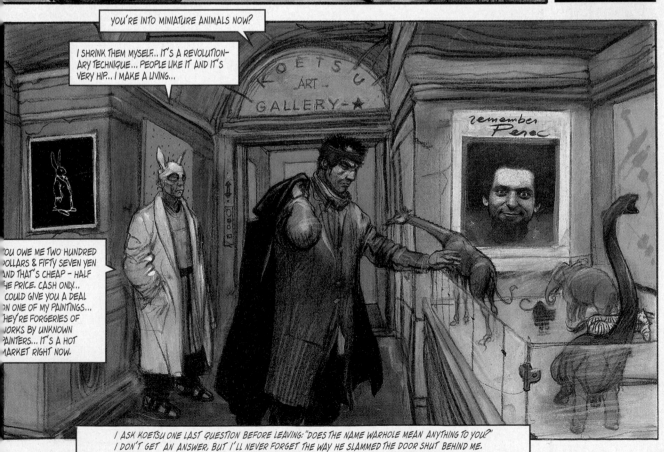

YOU'RE INTO MINIATURE ANIMALS NOW?

I SHRINK THEM MYSELF... IT'S A REVOLUTION-ARY TECHNIQUE... PEOPLE LIKE IT AND IT'S VERY HIP... I MAKE A LIVING...

OU OWE ME TWO HUNDRED OLLARS & FIFTY SEVEN YEN ND THAT'S CHEAP – HALF E PRICE. CASH ONLY... COULD GIVE YOU A DEAL N ONE OF MY PAINTINGS... HEY'RE FORGERIES OF ORKS BY UNKNOWN AINTERS... IT'S A HOT ARKET RIGHT NOW.

I ASK KOETSU ONE LAST QUESTION BEFORE LEAVING: "DOES THE NAME WARHOLE MEAN ANYTHING TO YOU?" I DON'T GET AN ANSWER, BUT I'LL NEVER FORGET THE WAY HE SLAMMED THE DOOR SHUT BEHIND ME.

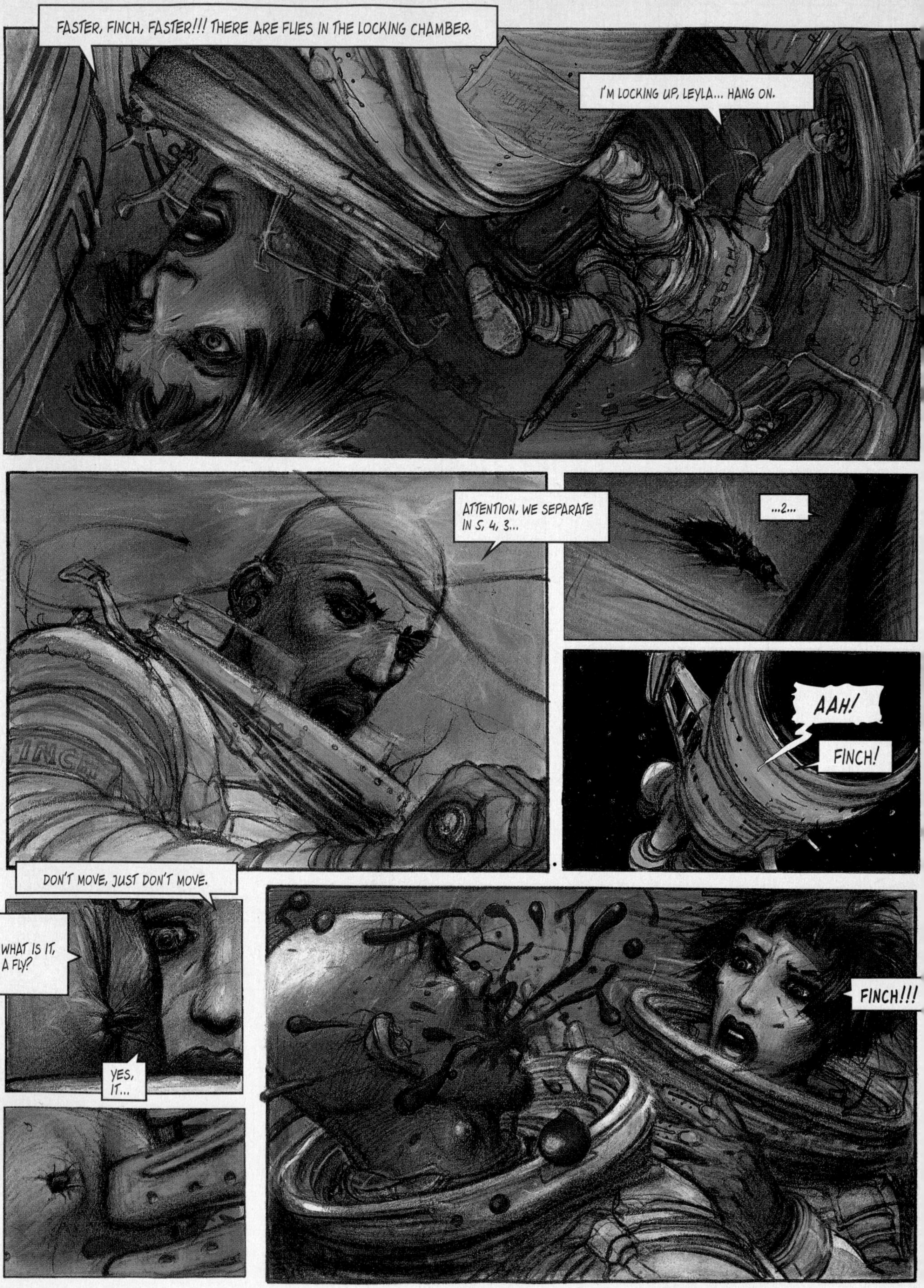
FASTER, FINCH, FASTER!!! THERE ARE FLIES IN THE LOCKING CHAMBER.
I'M LOCKING UP, LEYLA... HANG ON.
ATTENTION, WE SEPARATE IN 5, 4, 3...
...2...
AAH!
FINCH!
DON'T MOVE, JUST DON'T MOVE.
WHAT IS IT, A FLY?
YES, IT...
FINCH!!!

FIIIINCH!

D.12... I remember... Leyla's waving her pudgy little arms wildly. It takes me a while to realize she's fighting a huge black fly. The heat, of course... That day, two floors below us, a thirteen year old girl named Vesna, whose right arm and left hand have been amputated, tries to commit suicide. That same day, D.12, a shell smashes into one wing of the hospital, leaving behind three victims, one of which was a Sony television, unplugged and innocent.

I REALIZE LAZILY THAT WHILE THE MORPHINE SOOTHES MY PAIN, IT DOESN'T ALTER MY MEMORY FACULTIES. IN A FUZZY PAVLOVIAN WAY, I AM PERFECTLY AWARE OF WALKING BY THE CHRYSLER BUILDING, WHICH RECENTLY BURNED DOWN (WAS IT A TERRORIST ATTACK?)...

IT'S RIGHT THEN THAT, SUDDENLY, IN A FRACTION OF A SECOND, TEN THOUSAND NEEDLES JAB INTO THE HAND THAT'S BURIED IN MY LEFT POCKET.

HEY!?

FUCKIN' MINICAT!!!

I REMIND YOU THAT THIS CON-VERSATION IS NEITHER FILMED NOR RECORDED.

IS THAT CLEAR?

PERFECTLY CLEAR. I SUGGEST THAT DR. WARHOLE HIMSELF EXPLAIN THE NATURE OF HIS PROJECT.

IF A SINGLE PIECE OF INFORMATION EXCHANGED HERE TODAY WERE TO LEAK, WE'D ALL BE BROUGHT DOWN AND CONDEMNED.

I WOULD ALSO LIKE TO POINT OUT THAT, AS THE NO. 2 MAN FROM THE FBII, MY VERY PRESENCE HERE OFFICIALLY BEARS WITNESS TO THE BUREAU'S SPECIAL INTEREST IN THE DOCTOR'S WORK.

VERY WELL... GO AHEAD, DOCTOR.

PLEASE LISTEN CAREFULLY TO WHAT I'M ABOUT TO SAY. I DON'T LIKE TO REPEAT MYSELF

FOR THE GOOD OF THE PLANET, I SUGGEST THAT WE ONCE AND FOR ALL DESTROY THE OBSCURANTIS ORDER, ITS ERADICATOR BASE IN ORIENTAL SIBERIA, AS WELL AS THE THREE RECENTLY SELF-PROCLAIMED NUMBER ONES. ALL OF THIS MUST TAKE PLACE BEFORE THE EAGLE SITE HAS BEEN LOCATED AND ATTACKED AND BEFORE OTHER CRIMES ARE COMMITTED.

OH, IS THAT ALL?

I HAVE THE CAPABILITY AND I'D URGE YOU NOT TO DOUBT IT.

I WILL ARRANGE FOR SOMEONE TO BE "INTRODUCED" INTO THE CLOSED CIRCLE OF THE UNIONIST POWER AND THUS PINPOINT THE EXACT LOCATION OF THE SIBERIAN BASE. HE'S ONE OF THE CHOSEN ONES – THAT'S HOW THEY REFER TO THE MEN "SOUGHT" BY THE OBSCURANTIS ORDER. THIS MAN SEEMS TO BE OF GREAT INTEREST TO THE OBSCURANTISTS. THE FBII MANAGED TO RESUSCITATE HIM BY THE SKIN OF THEIR TEETH AND I WAS ABLE TO TAKE CARE OF HIM PERSONALLY. SPECIFICALLY, I'VE REMODELED HIS NOSE AND LINED HIS NASAL CAVITY WITH SELF-GUIDING MICRO-TRACKERS ATTUNED TO PARTICLE BEAM WEAPONS.

ONCE THE CHOSEN ONE HAS BEEN INTRODUCED INSIDE THEIR BASE, WE'LL SIMPLY DIRECT THE NECESSARY FIREPOWER FROM ONE OR MORE OF THE SATELLITES ORBITING THE EARTH.

I GUARANTEE THE UTTER AND COMPLETE DESTRUCTION OF THE OBSCURANTISTS' SITE AND OF ALL THE VERMIN NESTING WITHIN IT.

I MUST SAY, DOCTOR, I HAVE A HARD TIME TAKING YOUR PLAN SERIOUSLY.

IN ORDER TO CONTROL THE CHOSEN ONE AND OPTIMIZE HIS USE, I'VE PLANTED A RECEIVER IN HIS BRAIN. I'VE ALSO PLANTED A TRANSMITTER IN LIEUTENANT COBBEA'S BRAIN. THROUGH AN ACT OF EXTREME, CHEMICALLY SUSTAINED CONCENTRATION, LIEUTENANT COBBEA, PRESENT HERE, CAN INFLUENCE, UNDER MY DIRECTION, SOME OF THE SUBJECT'S BEHAVIOR. WE'LL BE ABLE TO MOVE THE CHOSEN ONE LIKE A CHESS PIECE BASED UPON OUR CHOSEN STRATEGY... THUS WILL HE WORK HIS WAY UP THE CHAIN OF THE OBSCURANTISTS UNTIL HE REACHES THEIR CORE.

HMMM... WHAT IS THE NAME OF THIS UNFORTUNATE CHOSEN ONE?

NIKE HATZFELD, A CBWM MEMORY SPECIALIST. HE'S AMONG THE FEW HUNDRED "IMPORTANT EXPENDABLES" ON THE U.N.'S CLASSIFICATION LIST. WE CAN AFFORD TO SACRIFICE HIM.

THERE'S SOMETHING I FIND TROUBLESOME IN YOUR SCENARIO, DOCTOR... WARHOLE? HAVE YOU SUBMITTED IT TO THE GOVERNING REPRESENTATIVES OF NATO...OR TO THE UNITED ARMIES FOR PEACE OR TO THE U.N. FOR THAT MATTER?

I COULDN'T CARE LESS ABOUT NATO, THE U.A.P OR THE INEFFECTUAL U.N.

WHAT IF I TOLD YOU, FOR EXAMPLE, THAT IN LESS THAN 10 SECONDS YOU ARE GOING TO RECEIVE A DIRECT CALL FROM THE HUBBLE STATION, WOULD YOU BELIEVE ME?

??!??

SPECIAL CALL, SIR.

D.11... I remember the night sky directly above me. Nothing particularly new, just a deluge of fire.
- I remember falling objects and traces of stars - the lament of daily death - I remember the routine, back and forth, of myself and Yelka, a nurse from Sarajevo.
Fat Yelka sings her French tune for the day as she changes me amidst the flies and then suddenly she falls on top of me, a trickle of blood perpendicular to her mouth.

WELL, MY FRIEND...HOW ARE THINGS ON HUBBLE?

WHAT IS THIS ALL ABOUT?!!? HUBBLE 4 HAS JUST BEEN ATTACKED.

THE STATION IS DOWN... I'M IN CONTACT WITH MODULE 3. THEY WERE ABLE TO DISENGAGE.

A DOCTOR! HURRY - FUCK!

ONE OF THE TWO CARETAKERS HAS BEEN INJURED AND THERE'S SOMETHING ABOUT FLIES.

LIKE THIS ONE?

CAN YOU HEAR ME ON EARTH? I NEED TO SPEAK TO A DOCTOR! A DOCTOR!

CALM DOWN, MISS. THIS IS DOCTOR OPTUS WARHOLE. CAN THE PATIENT STILL SPEAK?

FINCH

HE CAN'T HEAR ME ANYMORE. ALL HIS BLOOD IS SPILLING OUT. I'M BEGGING YOU, TELL ME WHAT I SHOULD DO.

I WILL EXPLAIN EVERYTHING, MISS... THE FLY IS IN THE PROCESS OF LAYING THOUSANDS OF EGGS ALONG THE VICTIM'S SPINAL COLUMN. THEY WILL EMBED THEMSELVES IN HIS ABDOMEN AND THEN IN HIS THORAX AND THEN MOVE UP TO HIS BRAIN. HE WILL SUFFER GREATLY AND DIE IN LESS THAN AN HOUR. THE LARVAE WILL FREE THEMSELVES IN NEARLY A WEEK. SINCE THESE FLIES ARE AN ELECTRONIC, ORGANIC, CHEMICAL AND EVEN VIRTUAL HYBRID, THERE'LL BE NO WAY TO DESTROY THEM. THERE IS ONLY ONE THING YOU CAN DO, MISS... EXPEL THE INFESTED BODY INTO SPACE!

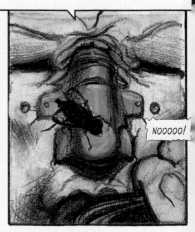

NOOOOO!

DOCTOR WARHOLE, ANSWER ME, WHAT'S THIS ALL ABOUT?

WHAT'S THE NAME OF THIS BRAVE YOUNG WOMAN, LOST, ALL ALONE, UP THERE IN SPACE?

DOES SHE KNOW THE LOCA— TION OF THE EAGLE SITE?

LEYLA MIRKOVIC-ZOHARY... A BRILLIANT ASTROPHYSICIST.

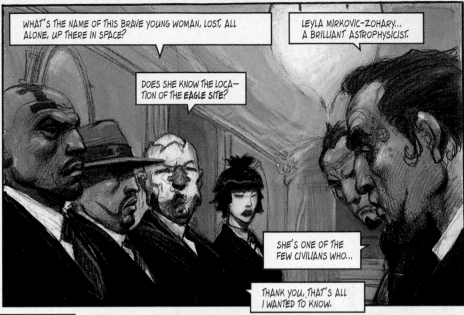

SHE'S ONE OF THE FEW CIVILIANS WHO...

THANK YOU, THAT'S ALL I WANTED TO KNOW.

DOCTOR WARHOLE!

YOUR BEHAVIOR IS INTOLERABLE! YOU'RE EXTORTING CLASSIFIED INFORMATION! I'D LIKE TO REMIND YOU THAT...

YOU NEED REMIND ME OF NOTHING. I GUARANTEE THAT IN LESS THAN THIRTY SECONDS ALL THAT'S BEEN SAID HERE WILL BE FORGOTTEN BY ALL OF YOU, FOREVER. THERE'S NOTHING LIKE DYING TO MAKE ONE FORGET, IS THERE?

WHAT ARE YOU TALKING ABOUT?

I'M TALKING ABOUT THE FACT THAT MY NASAL CAVITY, JUST LIKE THAT OF MY VERY DEAR CHOSEN ONE, NIKE, IS LINED WITH MICRO-TRACKERS FOR PARTICLE BEAM WEAPONS...

IF YOU FOLLOWED THE SCENARIO I LAID OUT YOU'LL HAVE UNDERSTOOD EVERYTHING... I'M ATTEMPTING A TEST ON A RATHER GRAND SCALE... THE LASER BEAM IS ON ITS WAY... MISS, GENTLEMEN, IF YOU ARE BELIEVERS, I SUGGEST YOU START SAYING YOUR PRAYERS...

YOU'RE MAD, WARHOLE!

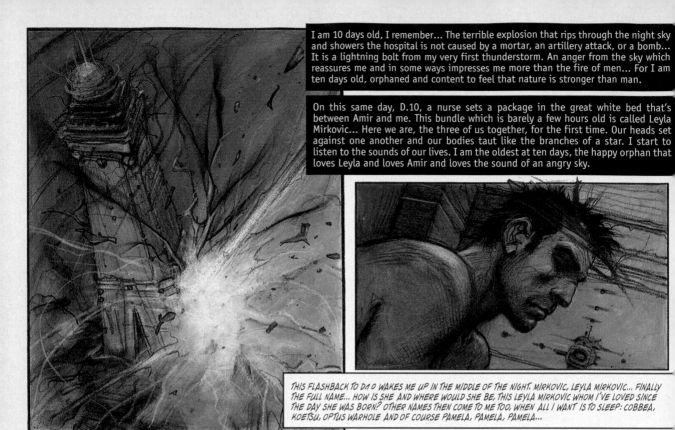

I am 10 days old, I remember... The terrible explosion that rips through the night sky and showers the hospital is not caused by a mortar, an artillery attack, or a bomb... It is a lightning bolt from my very first thunderstorm. An anger from the sky which reassures me and in some ways impresses me more than the fire of men... For I am ten days old, orphaned and content to feel that nature is stronger than man.

On this same day, D.10, a nurse sets a package in the great white bed that's between Amir and me. This bundle which is barely a few hours old is called Leyla Mirkovic... Here we are, the three of us together, for the first time. Our heads set against one another and our bodies taut like the branches of a star. I start to listen to the sounds of our lives. I am the oldest at ten days, the happy orphan that loves Leyla and loves Amir and loves the sound of an angry sky.

THIS FLASHBACK TO D.0 WAKES ME UP IN THE MIDDLE OF THE NIGHT. MIRKOVIC, LEYLA MIRKOVIC... FINALLY THE FULL NAME... HOW IS SHE AND WHERE WOULD SHE BE, THIS LEYLA MIRKOVIC WHOM I'VE LOVED SINCE THE DAY SHE WAS BORN? OTHER NAMES THEN COME TO ME TOO, WHEN ALL I WANT IS TO SLEEP: COBBEA, KOETSU, OPTUS WARHOLE AND OF COURSE PAMELA, PAMELA, PAMELA...

IT IS AT THIS PRECISE MOMENT THAT THE PAIN LEAVES MY SKULL AS IF A SWITCH IS FLIPPED AND I HEAR A VOICE – OR THE SHADOW OF A VOICE. SOMETHING THAT TAKES SHAPE AT THE VERY BOTTOM OF MY SKULL, WITHOUT TIMBRE OR COLOR AND SAYS AS ONE WORD, "BEWAREOFTHEREPLICATHEREPLICAISBORN." IT COMES IN CLEARLY: "BEWARE OF THE REPLICA. THE REPLICA IS BORN."???

I GET UP PUZZLED AND OBSESSED WITH COFFEE. I CATCH MINICAT'S EYE. SHE'S LAYING AMONGST THE CIGARETTE STUBS IN THE ASHTRAY. I THINK I HEAR HER PURRING.

SUCCESSFUL EJECTION-SUCCESSFUL EJECTION-SUCCESSFUL EJECTION...

40

ORIENTAL SIBERIA.

WAKE UP AMIR! AMIR! ALL OUR HAIR'S GONE! AMIIIIR!

CALM DOWN, MISS. MR. AMIR'S SLEEP WILL END IN 45 MINUTES, DON'T RUSH HIM.

WHO DID THIS TO US? WHO SHAVED OUR HEADS?

I'D LIKE TO POINT OUT THAT IN SPITE OF REPEATED WARNINGS, YOU AND THIS MAN COMMITTED AN ACT OF FORNICATION IN THIS VEHICLE...

AND NATURALLY THE SACRED FLY HAD TO REESTABLISH THE ESSENTIAL SPIRITUAL VALUES, IMPLEMENTING THE ERADICATOR'S FIRST LAW OF HYGENIC PURITY: NO MORE HAIR, NO PUBIC HAIR, NOTHING!

ARE YOU SAYING THAT THIS FILTHY INSECT...

GOD'S WORKER FULFILLED HIS DUTY.

FOR YOUR INFORMATION, WE WILL ARRIVE AT OUR DESTINATION TOMORROW AT DAWN.

NEW YORK. HEAD OFFICE OF THE CBMW.

FUCK YOU, MAN. WHAT THE HELL ARE YOU DOING HERE? I THOUGHT YOU WERE DEAD!

NEVER TRUST WHAT YOU READ IN THE PAPERS...

PARIS

OBSCURANTIST MADNESS STRIKES THE EIFFEL TOWER

Confirmation was received twelve hours after the attack that the Restricted Planetary Security Council was indeed the target of the deadly beam fired by a high altitude bomber.

Apart from the four permanent members of the Council, including acting President Paul Favier, the identification of victims, although extremely difficult, has been completed, confirming the deaths of Jeremy Preston, Number 2 at the F.B.I.I., as well as one of its agents, Ella Kyoniko. The "remains" of two unidentifiable android beings who were part of this clandestine and unsanctioned assembly are still wrapped in mystery. Certain leaks have indicated that one of the two androids was partially made up of living cells (fragments of lower limbs) belonging to the controversial Doctor Optus Warhole. This information would seem to confirm his very recent liaison with the F.B.I.I. The second floor of the famous Parisian monument was partially destroyed. Reconstruction work will begin and in order to

41

I HAVE TWO FAVORS TO ASK YOU, JAK.

FIRST, OBVIOUSLY YOU NEVER SAW ME. NEXT, LET ME LOOK SOMETHING UP ON THE GREAT COMPUTER. I JUST NEED TO ACCESS THE INTERNATIONAL PHONE DIRECTORY... SILLY THING REALLY, NO RISKS...

ARE YOU REALLY GOING TO STOP ME FROM INVESTIGATING MY OWN DEATH?

YOU KNOW THE RULES, NIKE... IF I GET—

ACCORDING TO THE GREAT COMPUTER, OF THE 3,000 MIRKOVICS LISTED IN THE WORLD, THERE ARE THREE LEYLAS. ONLY ONE OF THEM IS A "POSSIBLE," BORN IN 1993, REGISTERED IN THE TRIPLE-LOCKED RED LIST AND LIVING IN SARAJEVO! SO, LEYLA WENT BACK TO HER CITY...OUR CITY. THE COMPUTER IS IDEAL FOR CIRCUMVENTING OBSTACLES. IT UNLOCKS THE EXACT ADDRESS AND PRESTO, I GET THE NAME **ZOHARY**, LEYLA MIRKOVIC-**ZOHARY**, ASTROPHYSICIST. I TRY TO IMAGINE THE SCENE. LEYLA, WITH HER HEAD IN THE STARS... THE ROOFLESS HOSPITAL OF HER BIRTH MUST'VE GIVEN HER IDEAS.

YOU'RE VERY LUCKY. THE THREE NUMBER ONES ARE PRESENT... YOU MIGHT HAVE THE HONOR OF BEING INDUCTED BY THEM...

... WE MUST NEVER GET SEPARATED, NEVER...

I'M COLD, AMIR. I'M COLD AND I'M AFRAID. I'VE NEVER BEEN THIS COLD AND THIS AFRAID IN MY LIFE... THIS IS ALL MY FAULT.

WE HAVE TO STAY TOGETHER, NO MATTER WHAT.

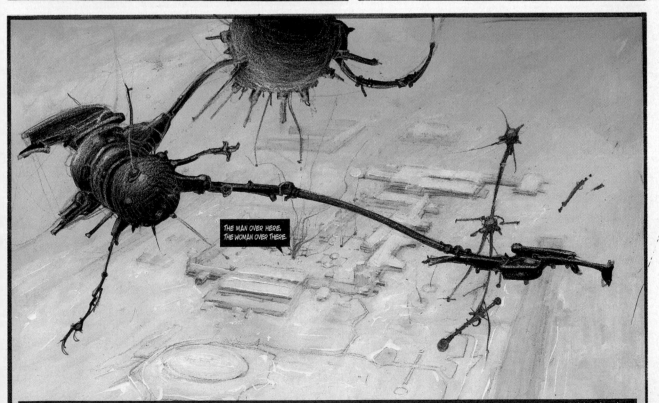

THE MAN OVER HERE, THE WOMAN OVER THERE.

D.9... I remember hearing the names of the camps: OMARSKA (closed down iron mine - Serb-controlled)... TRNOPOLJE (old school - Serb - controlled)... BILECA (student dormitory - Serb - controlled)... PALE (sports hall, and old movie theatre - Serb - controlled)... BRCKO (hangars- Serb-controlled)... ZVORNIK (stadium - Serb-controlled)... LIVNO (police station and school - Croatian-controlled)... BOSANSKI BROD (hangars - Croatian - controlled) TOMISLAVGRAD (school - Croatian - controlled) LJUBUSKI (Croatian - controlled)... KONJIC (sports hall - Bosnian - controlled)... BIHAC (Bosnian - controlled)... VISOKO (Bosnian - controlled)...

SACHA IRINA KRYLOVA, NUMBER 44-766... PURSUANT TO OUR INVESTIGATION AND TO CUT TO THE HEART OF THE MATTER, WE KNOW THAT YOU WERE BORN IN THE YEAR 2003 IN SOTCHI... THAT YOU LEAVE THE FAMILY UNIT AT THE AGE OF 6 WITHOUT RECEIVING THE SLIGHTEST RELIGIOUS EDUCATION... THAT YOU SOON TURN INTO AN ACTIVE DELINQUENT – 6.7 OUT OF 10...

...THAT YOU STEAL, THAT YOU ARE INVOLVED IN THE TRAFFIC OF HALLUCINOGENIC POWDERS, THAT YOU KILL, THAT YOU FORNICATE... THAT YOU STEAL AGAIN, THAT YOU...

I'D LIKE TO POINT OUT THAT THE HOMICIDES WERE CASES OF SELF-DEFENSE!

BOW YOUR HEAD WHEN YOU SPEAK.

... AS I WAS SAYING... THAT YOU STEAL AGAIN, THAT YOU GO ON TRAFFICKING IN HALLUCINATORY POWDERS, KILLING, FORNICATING, AND SO ON... ALL TOGETHER, YOUR 23 YEARS OF LIFE ARE A MISERABLE FAILURE.

YOU DID WELL TO COME TO US.

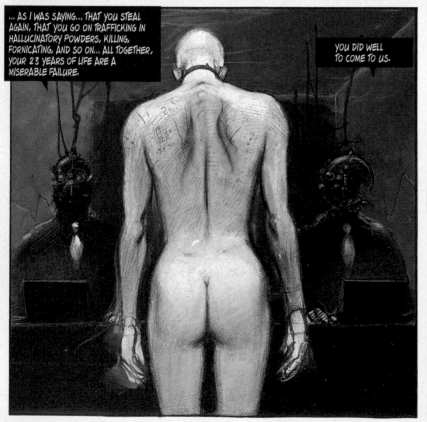

PERHAPS I DID, BUT THE CONTRACT I SIGNED IN MOSCOW HAD NOTHING TO DO WITH THIS CHARADE.

YOU MUST HAVE BEEN DREAMING, NO. 44-766. ONE DOESN'T SIGN A CONTRACT WITH THE OBSCURANTIS ORDER, ONE SUBMITS.

I REPEAT, AMIR FAZLAGIC AND I WERE HIRED AS A TEAM. WE'RE TOGETHER AND WE...

THE NOTION OF COUPLES OR INDIVIDUALS MEANS NOTHING HERE, MISS 44-766. SO, SINCE YOU'VE ALREADY BEEN SHAVED/PURIFIED, I SUGGEST YOU PROCEED IMMEDIATELY TO THE SINGLE UNIT WELCOME CHAMBER... YOU'LL SEE, EVERYTHING WILL BE QUITE DIFFERENT TOMORROW. YOU CAN'T IMAGINE HOW MUCH... GOOD NIGHT AND MAY YOUR FINAL DREAMS BE SWEET. **NEXT ERADICATOR!**

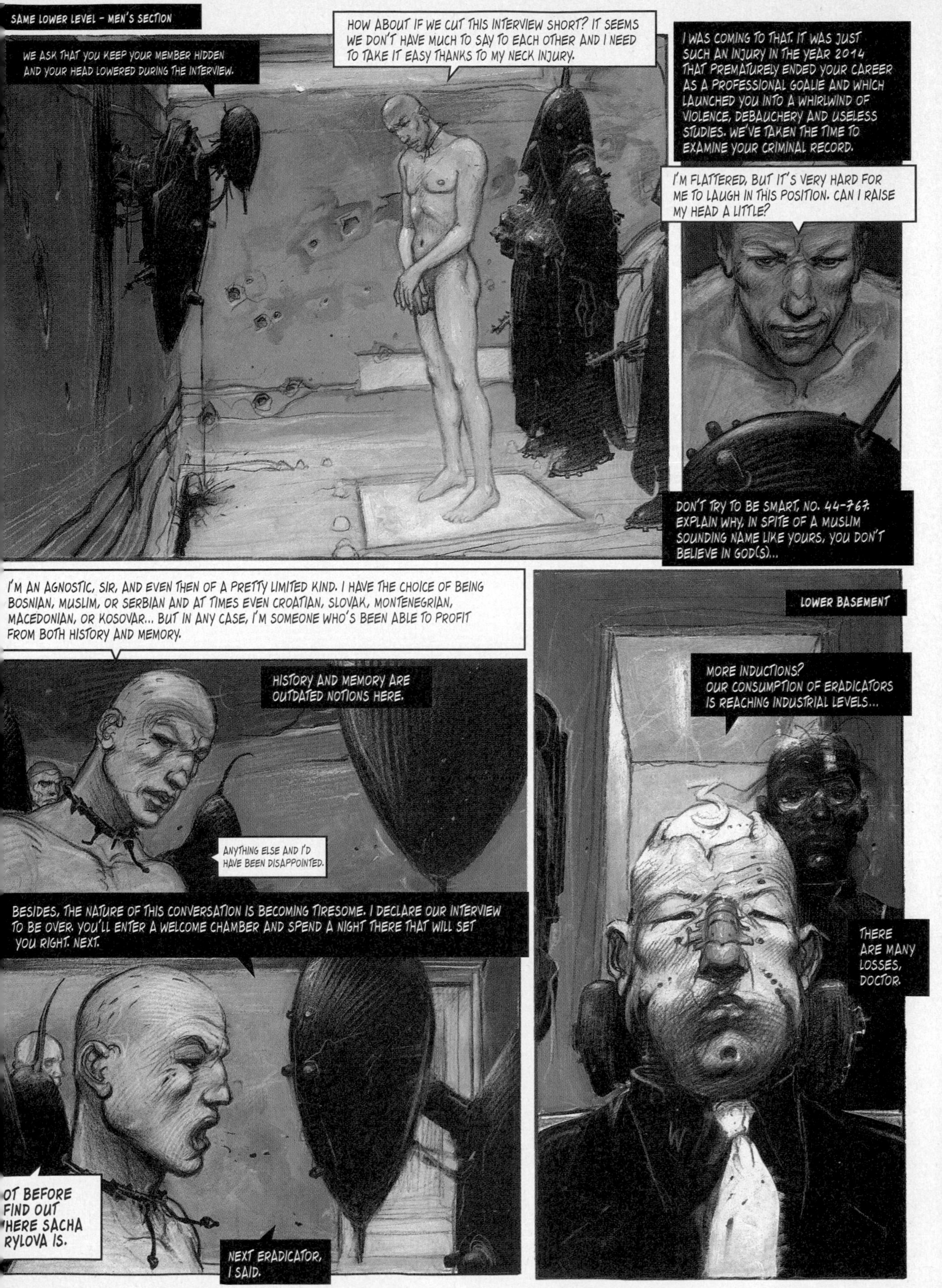
SAME LOWER LEVEL - MEN'S SECTION
WE ASK THAT YOU KEEP YOUR MEMBER HIDDEN AND YOUR HEAD LOWERED DURING THE INTERVIEW.
HOW ABOUT IF WE CUT THIS INTERVIEW SHORT? IT SEEMS WE DON'T HAVE MUCH TO SAY TO EACH OTHER AND I NEED TO TAKE IT EASY THANKS TO MY NECK INJURY.
I WAS COMING TO THAT. IT WAS JUST SUCH AN INJURY IN THE YEAR 2014 THAT PREMATURELY ENDED YOUR CAREER AS A PROFESSIONAL GOALIE AND WHICH LAUNCHED YOU INTO A WHIRLWIND OF VIOLENCE, DEBAUCHERY AND USELESS STUDIES. WE'VE TAKEN THE TIME TO EXAMINE YOUR CRIMINAL RECORD.
I'M FLATTERED, BUT IT'S VERY HARD FOR ME TO LAUGH IN THIS POSITION. CAN I RAISE MY HEAD A LITTLE?
DON'T TRY TO BE SMART, NO. 44-767. EXPLAIN WHY, IN SPITE OF A MUSLIM SOUNDING NAME LIKE YOURS, YOU DON'T BELIEVE IN GOD(S)...
I'M AN AGNOSTIC, SIR, AND EVEN THEN OF A PRETTY LIMITED KIND. I HAVE THE CHOICE OF BEING BOSNIAN, MUSLIM, OR SERBIAN AND AT TIMES EVEN CROATIAN, SLOVAK, MONTENEGRIAN, MACEDONIAN, OR KOSOVAR... BUT IN ANY CASE, I'M SOMEONE WHO'S BEEN ABLE TO PROFIT FROM BOTH HISTORY AND MEMORY.
HISTORY AND MEMORY ARE OUTDATED NOTIONS HERE.
ANYTHING ELSE AND I'D HAVE BEEN DISAPPOINTED.
BESIDES, THE NATURE OF THIS CONVERSATION IS BECOMING TIRESOME. I DECLARE OUR INTERVIEW TO BE OVER. YOU'LL ENTER A WELCOME CHAMBER AND SPEND A NIGHT THERE THAT WILL SET YOU RIGHT. NEXT.
OT BEFORE FIND OUT HERE SACHA RYLOVA IS.
NEXT ERADICATOR, I SAID.
LOWER BASEMENT
MORE INDUCTIONS? OUR CONSUMPTION OF ERADICATORS IS REACHING INDUSTRIAL LEVELS...
THERE ARE MANY LOSSES, DOCTOR.

AND MY DEAR ASSOCIATES, NOS. 1 AND 2? I THOUGHT THEY WERE IN A HURRY TO MEET WITH ME.

THE FLY, BEWARE OF THE FLY.

THEY ARE RECUP-ERATING FROM THEIR VERY LONG JOURNEY.

ARE YOU SAYING THAT WE'RE TOO FAR FROM EVERYTHING OUT HERE?

?!?

IN ANY NEW YORKER'S MEMORY AND, WITH ALL MODESTY, IN MINE IN PARTICULAR, THERE HADN'T BEEN SUCH GLORIOUS WEATHER IN CENTRAL PARK FOR OVER TWO DECADES. EVEN THE LITTLE MINICAT IN MY HAND COULDN'T GET OVER IT.

IN A FEW DAYS, MINICAT, I'LL BE IN SARAJEVO... PERHAPS RIGHT IN FRONT OF LEYLA... IF YOU WANT, I'LL TAKE YOU...

D.8... I remember. The heat and the stench of death. And the inarticulate gestures of Amir, who is haphazardly kicking and boxing the air that is infested with the very same flies day after day... Today, they're as big as my hand.
Next to us I hear an escapee from the camps confiding, between sobs, to fat Yelka: "What can one say when a guard beats a prisoner only to take him in his arms, embrace him and cry?"
In the distance, there is an offensive on Mount Igman.

THIS FLASHBACK, IN WHICH LEYLA IS NATURALLY ABSENT, SINCE SHE IS UNBORN AT THIS POINT, QUICKLY FADES OUT, LEAVING ROOM FOR SOMETHING HEAVIER STILL. THE INEXPRESSIBLE SHADOW OF A VOICE, ONCE AGAIN BORING ITS WAY THROUGH THE RESISTANT SYNAPSES OF MY BRAIN, FROM WHICH ONLY THE MEREST TRACE OF A WHISPER WOULD SURVIVE: ... PAMELA FISHERHASBEENFOUND... ...PAMELAFISHERHAS-BEENFOUND... PAMELA FISHER HAS BEEN FOUND.

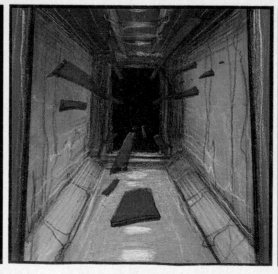

– YOU'RE PLACING US IN DANGER, WARHOLE! YOUR UNILATERAL DECISIONS ARE UNACCEPTABLE!

– YOU PUT ME IN CHARGE OF THE DESTRUCTION OF THE EAGLE SITE. I'LL CONDUCT MY INQUIRY AND TEST MY WEAPONS AS I SEE FIT.

– I REPEAT THAT I CONSIDER THE ATTACK ON THE EIFFEL TOWER USELESS AND DANGEROUS.

– NUMBER 2 IS RIGHT. . . I ALSO FAIL TO COMPLETELY UNDERSTAND THE MEANING OF YOUR . . . EXCESSIVE ACTION.

– IN TERMS OF EXCESSES AND ERADICATIONS OF EVERY KIND, I FIND I'M FAR INFERIOR TO YOU, DEAR NUMBER ONE. BUT I'LL EXPLAIN.

– GO AHEAD, EXPLAIN...

– IF I SENT MY LATEST DOUBLE TO PARIS, IT WAS...

– I'M BEGINNING TO FIND YOUR "DOUBLE" STORIES TROUBLESOME, DR. WARHOLE. WHO KNOWS, FOR INSTANCE, WHETHER YOU'RE THE ORIGINAL? IT APPEARS THAT TRACES OF YOUR BODY WERE FOUND AT THE SITE OF THE ATTACK.

I LIKE TO GIVE EACH OF MY DOUBLES A PIECE OF MY OWN BODY. IT IS PART OF MY PERSONAL CODE OF ETHICS.

IN THIS CASE, IT WAS MY OLD LEGS, WHICH HAD RECENTLY TURNED GANGRENOUS AND WHICH I AMPUTATED MYSELF.

BUT, ALLOW ME TO CONTINUE. AT THE TIME OF THIS PARISIAN MEETING, WHICH WAS TO HAVE BEEN QUITE MUNDANE, MY LAST DOUBLE OBTAINED VITAL INFORMATION REGARDING THE LOCATION OF THE EAGLE SITE. THEREFORE, I CAN NOW GUARANTEE THE IMMINENT DESTRUCTION OF THE SITE, WHICH MAY I REMIND YOU, OBSESSES YOU MUCH MORE THAN IT DOES ME. WHETHER GOD DOES OR DOES NOT EXIST IS ONE OF MY LESSER WORRIES, AS YOU KNOW. SO YOU SHOULD, ON THE CONTRARY, PRAISE MY EXTRAORDINARY EFFICIENCY.

WHAT WAS THE INFORMATION YOU DISCOVERED?

A NAME, A MERE NAME.

- THAT OF SOMEONE FROM THE INSIDE. A MINOR ASTROPHYSICIST, BUT ONE WHO KNOWS THE LOCATION, THE EXACT LOCATION OF THE SITE. ALL WE NEEDED WAS TO KNOW WHERE TO STRIKE. WELL, I'LL KNOW VERY SOON... I MANAGED TO KILL THREE BIRDS WITH ONE STONE. FIRST, I ELIMINATED ALL THE WITNESSES PRESENT AT THAT MEETING, WHICH WAS ESSENTIAL, THOUGH THIS UNFORTUNATELY INCLUDED MY DOUBLE, AS WELL AS THE DUPLICATE OF MY FAITHFUL COBBEA. SECONDLY, I WAS ABLE TO TEST THE EFFICIENCY OF THE SATELLITE-LASER SYSTEM DEVELOPED TO DESTROY THE SITE. AND FINALLY, THE THIRD ACCOMPLISHMENT, WHICH WAS REWARDING ON A PERSONAL LEVEL, WAS INFLICTING DAMAGE ON A MONUMENT WHICH, EVER SINCE I WAS LITTLE, HAS REALLY BOTHERED ME. YOU KNOW I'M BOTH A CHESS PLAYER AND A GAMBLER, EVEN IN RESEARCH AND MEDICINE... I'M A LUNATIC WEAVING AWAY AND IT'S ALWAYS SUCCEEDED FOR ME...

- I IMAGINE YOU ARE NO LONGER IN THE F.B.I.I.'S GOOD GRACES...

THE F.B.I.I. WAS NO LONGER USEFUL TO ME... IN ANY CASE, I THINK I'VE DEFINITIVELY EARNED THE RIGHT TO BE NUMBER ONE OF THE OBSCURANTIS ORDER...

WE DO NOT QUESTION YOUR EFFICIENCY, NOR ALAS, THE EFFICACY OF YOUR SCATTERSHOT LUNACY... BUT WE MUST ASK YOU NOT TO FORGET THAT YOU'RE ONLY NUMBER THREE... THERE ARE TWO OF US BEFORE YOU... AND WE'LL AWAIT THE RESULTS OF YOUR ERADICATION OF THE EAGLE SITE. THAT IS OF UTMOST URGENCY.

WE GIVE YOU ONE WEEK AND NOT A DAY LONGER.

D.7... I remember the sky set ablaze by sunrise and by the fire of men. Do flies have ears? If so, were the Sarajevo flies deafened by the sounds of war? For they are there, descending from the sky that opens onto hell, clumsy and slow in their flight. For once they can't be heard. Not even when they buzz right by your ear. Then I remember Amir, behind my back, focused like never before, his shoulder quivering, about to strike...

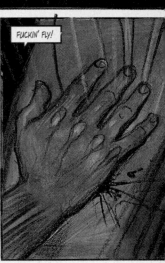

FUCKIN' FLY!

D.7 continued - A squashed fly is like an abstract painting. The one in Amir's hand is his proud trophy and makes him laugh in short bursts against the background roar of the explosions. It could look like a sick flower, or a mutant crab, or a celestial object, a reflection in a de-forming mirror, the smile of an ethnic cleanser, or a poorly cooked burek, or a bad baklava, or a zealous media intellectual, or a decree from the United Nations Security Council, or an aerial view of a wounded city... I grab Amir's hand and look at its sullied palm. There I see Sarajevo, dying.

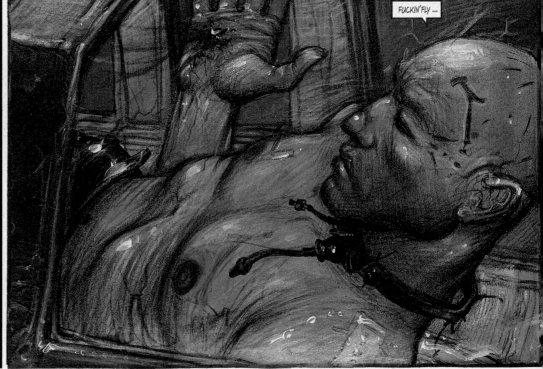

FUCKIN'FLY ...

E NEFOUD DESERT.

THIS IS MY MOST BEAUTIFUL TOY, LEYLA, AND IT'S ALSO MY LAST ONE... AND I OWE IT TO YOU.

THIS GIFT COMES FROM FINCH AS WELL... HE OBTAINED ALL OF THE NECESSARY CLEARANCES BEFORE HE DIED...

BUT IT'S A DANGEROUS TOY, DAD.

EVEN THOUGH THE ANTI-INERTIA SYSTEM IS EFFICIENT... THE CABLE WILL REACH AN ALTITUDE OF 36,000 METERS ONCE IT'S EXTENDED.... BUT GOING OVER 20,000 WOULD BE RISKY FOR YOU...

YOU MUST LET ME USE IT THE WAY I SEE FIT, LEYLA... SO LONG AS I CAN SEE...

AT 102, I'M WELL OVER 21... DON'T BREAK OUR PACT.

...LET US REMAIN WHAT WE ALWAYS WERE... FREE PEOPLE... IT'S BECOME SO RARE THAT WE SHOULD CLING TO IT... AT LEAST TO THE IDEA OF IT... AND I WANT TO BE FREE EVEN IN THE CHOICE OF MY OWN DEATH. YOU KNOW THAT IN MY POLITICAL LIFE, I BELIEVE I WAS TRULY OF SERVICE ONLY ONCE, WHEN, EARLY IN THE CENTURY, I BROUGHT ABOUT THE ISRAELI-PALESTINIAN PEACE... YOU WEREN'T EVEN 10 AND I'D JUST ADOPTED YOU... TODAY, BECAUSE OF RAMPANT OBSCURANTISM, THE PEACE IS ONCE AGAIN FALLING APART AND I CAN DO NOTHING ABOUT IT... I WANT TO LEAVE THIS WORLD OF MEN WITH GRACE AND ELEGANCE... AT 36,000 METERS. CAN YOU IMAGINE? LIKE A FEATHER...

I KNEW I'D HAVE TO HEAR THIS ONE DAY. I LOST FINCH AND NOW IT'S YOU WHO...

DON'T DISAPPOINT ME, LEYLA...ABOVE ALL DON'T BE DISTRAUGHT. OUR PACT DOESN'T ALLOW SUCH TALK...

NOW WILL YOU HAVE A DRINK WITH ME? TO MY ELEVATOR TO THE STARS, OF COURSE, AND TO US...FOREVER.

BASEMENT 3.

CAN YOU HEAR ME, COBBEA? LIEUTENANT COBBEA?

...HEAR...

I MUST ACT MORE QUICKLY THAN I'D FORESEEN. I'LL ASK YOU A FEW QUESTIONS AND DICTATE SOME NEW ELEMENTS... ARE YOU READY?

...READY.

AT THIS PRECISE MOMENT, WHERE IS OUR CHOSEN ONE, NIKE HATZFELD?

AIR FRANCE FLIGHT 997...DESTINATION SARAJEVO...BUSINESS CLASS.

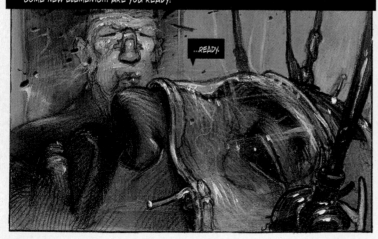

50

VERY WELL... WERE YOUR LAST TESTS WITH HIM CONCLUSIVE?
CAN YOU SCAN HIS NEURONS EFFECTIVELY AND DOES HE OBEY OUR COMMANDS?

... POSITIVE RESULTS...
SATISFACTORY...

- LAST TEST CONCLUSIVE?

- ... TEST IN PROGRESS... REPETITIVE SIMULATION
OF INCONTINENCE... RESULTS VERY CONVINCING...

- PERFECT. I WOULD LIKE TO LAUNCH THE OPERATION
QUICKLY...DO YOU FEEL YOU CAN GET THE RESULTS
WE NEED? I MEAN IS YOUR ABILITY TO CONCENTRATE
AT ITS OPTIMUM LEVEL? DO YOU NEED ANYTHING?

- ... OPTIMAL...AM READY... NEED NOTHING...

- GOOD. HERE ARE THE NEW ELEMENTS THAT I WOULD LIKE YOU TO RECORD.
THE INCOMPLETE DOUBLE OF NIKE HATZFELD IS BEING SENT TO SARAJEVO TODAY UNDER FLY CONTROL... PLUG THE AFOREMENTIONED DOUBLE INTO THE ORIGINAL NIKE
HATZFELD IN ORDER TO COMPLETE INITIALIZATION (WHAT INTERESTS ME MOST IS HIS MEMORY CAPACITY)... THE DOUBLE MUST BE RETURNED TO US HERE IMMEDIATELY;
AND THE ORIGINAL IS TO GO, WITH AN EMBEDDED FLY, TO THE ASTROPHYSICIST MIRKOVIC-ZOHARY... THE DESTINATION SEEMS TO BE THE NEFOUD DESERT (WE WILL PINPOINT
THE EXACT LOCATION). NOTE, SHE'LL BE AT THE HOUSE OF HER ADOPTIVE FATHER, THE FORMER MINISTER OF FOREIGN AFFAIRS FOR THE STATE OF ISRAEL, SHIMON ZOHARY.
I HAVE REASON TO BELIEVE THAT WE WILL NOT BE VERY FAR FROM THE EAGLE SITE. THE FLY WILL BE ASSIGNED TO FINDING THE PRECISE LOCATION AND THEN
ALL I'LL NEED TO DO IS MAKE OUR PAWN NIKE GO THERE FOR THE LAST STRIKE AND THE FINAL FIREWORKS. . .
DOES THIS PLAN-SYNOPSIS WORK FOR YOU, COBBEA?

- ... WORKS... ELEMENTS RECORDED... AM READY...

I MUST ASK YOU A PERSONAL QUESTION, COBBEA.
DO YOU BELIEVE ME TO BE TRULY EVIL?

... BELIEVE YOU...
TRULY ...

YOUR HONESTY TOUCHES MY HEART. I'LL SEND PAMELA FISHER
TO FILL YOU IN ON THE DETAILS.

AF FLIGHT 997.

IF YOU HAVE A PROBLEM, SIR, THE DOCTOR ON BOARD CAN HELP YOU...
SHOULD I CALL HIM?

A DOCTOR? WHY?

I DON'T KNOW, SIR, BUT YOU'VE BEEN GOING TO THE REST-
ROOM EVERY OTHER MINUTE FOR THE LAST FIFTEEN MINUTES...

ANOTHER DAY.

SACHA...

IT'S ME, AMIR.

SACHA?

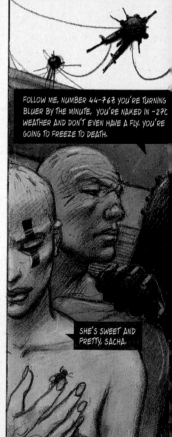

FOLLOW ME, NUMBER 44-767. YOU'RE TURNING BLUER BY THE MINUTE. YOU'RE NAKED IN -27°C WEATHER AND DON'T EVEN HAVE A FLY. YOU'RE GOING TO FREEZE TO DEATH.

SQUASH THAT FUCKING THING, SACHA... I BEG YOU...

SHE'S SWEET AND PRETTY, SACHA.

LOOK AT ME.

LET ME INTRODUCE MY FLY. SHE'S CALLED SACHA AND I TOO AM CALLED SACHA.

WHAT'S YOUR FLY CALLED?

52

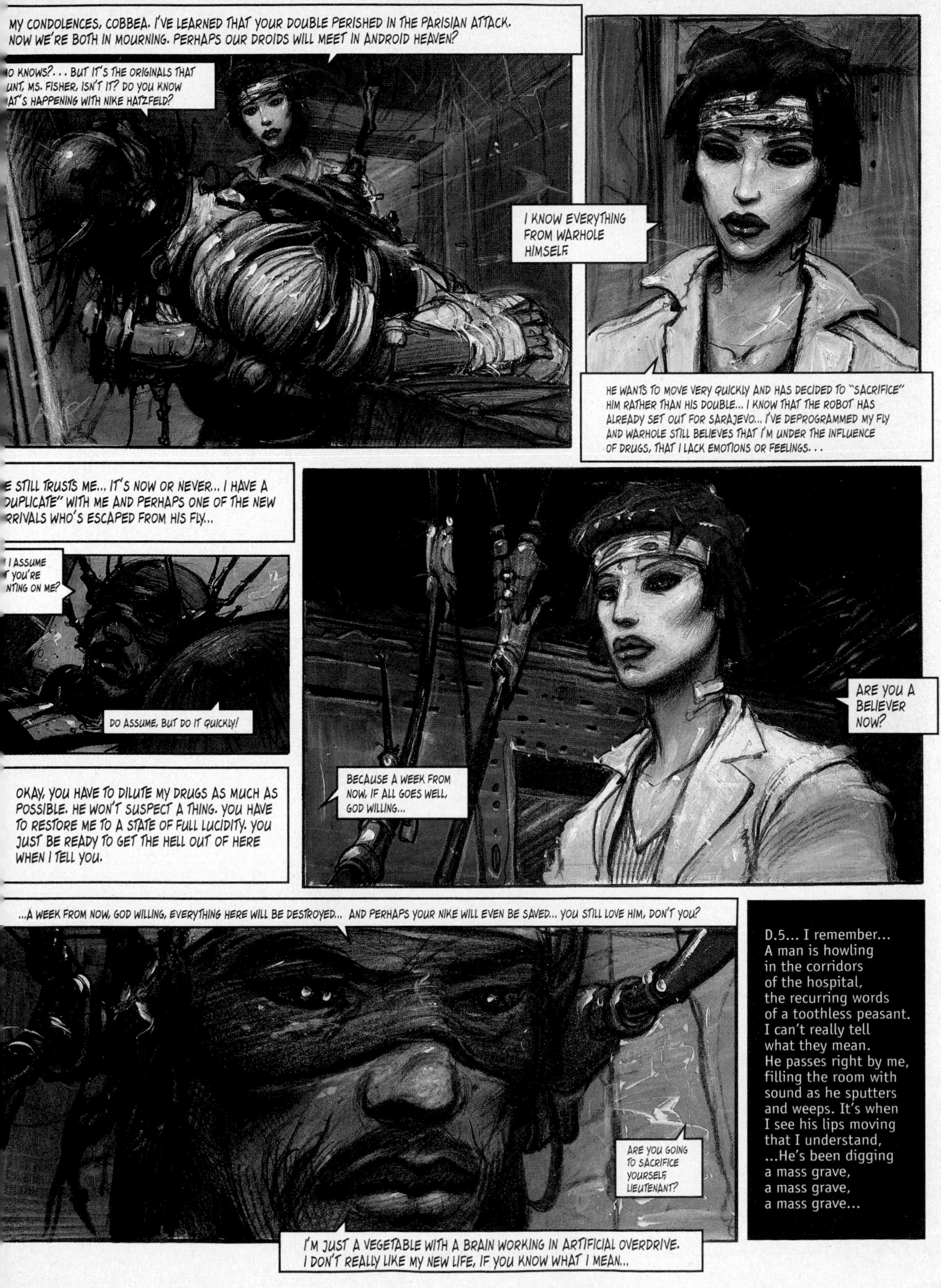
MY CONDOLENCES, COBBEA. I'VE LEARNED THAT YOUR DOUBLE PERISHED IN THE PARISIAN ATTACK. NOW WE'RE BOTH IN MOURNING. PERHAPS OUR DROIDS WILL MEET IN ANDROID HEAVEN?
O KNOWS?. . . BUT IT'S THE ORIGINALS THAT UNT, MS. FISHER, ISN'T IT? DO YOU KNOW AT'S HAPPENING WITH NIKE HATZFELD?
I KNOW EVERYTHING FROM WARHOLE HIMSELF.
HE WANTS TO MOVE VERY QUICKLY AND HAS DECIDED TO "SACRIFICE" HIM RATHER THAN HIS DOUBLE... I KNOW THAT THE ROBOT HAS ALREADY SET OUT FOR SARAJEVO... I'VE DEPROGRAMMED MY FLY AND WARHOLE STILL BELIEVES THAT I'M UNDER THE INFLUENCE OF DRUGS, THAT I LACK EMOTIONS OR FEELINGS. . .
E STILL TRUSTS ME... IT'S NOW OR NEVER... I HAVE A DUPLICATE" WITH ME AND PERHAPS ONE OF THE NEW RRIVALS WHO'S ESCAPED FROM HIS FLY...
I ASSUME YOU'RE NTING ON ME?
DO ASSUME, BUT DO IT QUICKLY!
OKAY, YOU HAVE TO DILUTE MY DRUGS AS MUCH AS POSSIBLE. HE WON'T SUSPECT A THING. YOU HAVE TO RESTORE ME TO A STATE OF FULL LUCIDITY. YOU JUST BE READY TO GET THE HELL OUT OF HERE WHEN I TELL YOU.
BECAUSE A WEEK FROM NOW, IF ALL GOES WELL, GOD WILLING...
ARE YOU A BELIEVER NOW?
...A WEEK FROM NOW, GOD WILLING, EVERYTHING HERE WILL BE DESTROYED... AND PERHAPS YOUR NIKE WILL EVEN BE SAVED... YOU STILL LOVE HIM, DON'T YOU?
ARE YOU GOING TO SACRIFICE YOURSELF, LIEUTENANT?
I'M JUST A VEGETABLE WITH A BRAIN WORKING IN ARTIFICIAL OVERDRIVE. I DON'T REALLY LIKE MY NEW LIFE, IF YOU KNOW WHAT I MEAN...
D.5... I remember... A man is howling in the corridors of the hospital, the recurring words of a toothless peasant. I can't really tell what they mean. He passes right by me, filling the room with sound as he sputters and weeps. It's when I see his lips moving that I understand, ...He's been digging a mass grave, a mass grave, a mass grave...

THE CRY THAT I UNLEASH, 33 YEARS AFTER THE TOOTHLESS PEASANT OF MY MEMORIES, ON THE ROOF OF AN ORDINARY HOTEL IN THE CENTER OF SARAJEVO, IS INDESCRIBABLE.

THIS MUNCHIAN SCREAM IS THE FIRST SOUND I'VE UTTERED SINCE MY RETURN TO THE TOWN OF MY BIRTH. BUT IT FLEES MY MOUTH ABRUPTLY AND IS QUICKLY STIFLED IN THE HUMID AIR OF THE NEW RELIGIOUS DISTRICT... TO SCREAM IN A CITY WHICH HAS DROWNED IN MEMORIES OF BOMBS AND DEATH IS RIDICULOUS, PATHETIC, USELESS...

THE "DUPLICATES" IN HOODS ARE THE PARTIAL DOUBLES OF THE ERADICATORS. THEY'RE SUPPOSED TO STAY IN THE BASE AND THEIR MEANS ARE LIMITED, BUT THIS ONE WILL HELP US. ACCORDING TO HIM, THERE IS ONLY ONE SOLUTION...

YES, THE ONLY POSSIBILITY IS TO TAKE ONE OF THE "SMART" VEHICLES. THEY HAVE NO DRIVERS AND SINCE I'M A "DUPLICATE" THESE ARE THE ONLY ONES I CAN START... AS FOR OUR DESTINATION, THAT, AS WELL AS EVERYTHING ELSE, WILL BE DETERMINED BY LUCK.

ONCE I GET THE MESSAGE FROM COBBEA, WE'LL HAVE TO MOVE FAST. I ADVISE YOU TO COME WITH US, MR. AMIR FAZLAGIC... YOU DON'T DESERVE TO STAY HERE.

I MUST SAVE SACHA KRYLOVA.

– FORGET NUMBER 44-766... THE NEW ERADICATOR UNIT HAS BEEN CONSTITUTED... YOUR FRIEND HAS BEEN INTEGRATED INTO A 3 MEMBER FEMALE TEAM THAT HAS ALREADY BEGUN TRAINING AND UNDERTAKING MISSIONS. SHE, LIKE EVERYONE ELSE HERE, IS BEING CONTROLLED BY A FLY... OF ALL THOSE I'VE WARNED, YOU'RE THE ONLY ONE WHO'S BEEN FAST ENOUGH TO ELIMINATE ONE OF GOD'S WORKERS... YOU HAVE ASTOUNDING REFLEXES.

SLEEP IN ITS FIFTH STAGE, THE RAPID AND PARADOXICAL STAGE, IS AN ELUSIVE MONSTER... HOW CAN I REMEMBER THIS, THE FIRST OF MY SARAJEVO DREAMS? (AN IMPOSSIBLE SCREAM, OBVIOUSLY.) WEIGHED DOWN BY MY EXTREME CONFUSION, I WALK ONSTAGE, MY FOREHEAD HEAVILY CREASED LIKE A TORTURED SHARPEI, MY BACKDROP THE OPEN HOLE IN THE HOSPITAL CEILING WHOSE OUTLINE EVOKES THE COUNTRY THAT DIED AT MY BIRTH. HOW CAN I MAKE MYSELF CLEAR, EVEN TO MYSELF? IF MY PRODIGIOUS MEMORY HAS A WEAKNESS, IT'S ROOTED IN THESE ZONES OF SLEEP, SUSPENSION AND INERTIA, WHERE VIGILANCE IS NO LONGER...

IN THE MORNING, PIECES OF THIS DREAM COME FLOODING BACK AND ARE SLOWLY BROUGHT INTO FOCUS BY A "FAMILIAR" SHADOW OF A VOICE...COBBEA! IT'S COBBEA WHO'S BEEN "SPEAKING" TO ME! NOW I CAN HEAR HIM DISTINCTLY. HE'S CHATTERING IN MY BRAIN WITH THE INSISTENCE OF A STEREO SPEAKER. MY SYNAPSES GIVE UP QUICKLY AND, AS IF BY MAGIC, THE PAIN RETURNS.
COBBEA FEEDS ME ALL KINDS OF INFORMATION. OUR RESPECTIVE SURGICAL SETBACKS AND OUR FORCED TIES, MY NOSE "THE LASER MAGNET" AND WARHOLE THE OBSCURANTIST MONSTER, PAMELA, THE VICTIM OF LOVE, MY DOUBLE HEADING FOR ME AND FINALLY LEYLA... HERSELF A PAWN ON THE SAME INFERNAL CHESSBOARD, FAR FROM EVERYTHING, IN THE MIDDLE OF A DESERT, FAR FROM OUR SARAJEVO, FAR FROM ME... THE SOUND OF BELLS RINGING AND THE CHANT OF THE MUEZZIN...

I RENT A CAR AND FLY OVER SNIPER ALLEY TWO (2012 CONFLICT) FOR THE FIRST TIME IN MY LIFE.

RAMPANT OBSCURANTISM HAS ONCE AGAIN EMPTIED THE CITY OF ITS YOUTH... EVER SINCE THE DESTRUCTION OF THE FORMER YUGOSLAVIA IN THE LAST CENTURY, THE BALKANS REMAIN THE HYPER-LIBERAL INTERNATIONAL COMMUNITY'S FAVORITE LABORATORY. THE "SOFT" OBSCURANTISM WHICH IS TOLERATED (TESTED) NOW IS MEANT TO SHORT-CIRCUIT THE OTHER EXTREMIST TENDENCIES, INCLUDING THAT OF THE SELF-PROCLAIMED NUMBER ONES KNOWN TO MY "FRIEND" WARHOLE... I FIND MYSELF DRIVING VERY BADLY (PULLING TO THE LEFT AND FLYING TOO HIGH). COBBEA'S BRUTAL INVASION OF MY BRAIN SEEMS TO HAVE EXACERBATED VARIOUS PAINS AND BRUISES... DOES THIS MEAN THE BRAIN IS A MUSCLE?

D.4... A story is making the rounds at the hospital... Sniper Alley's most resourceful and twisted sniper, having learned of his wife's death at childbirth, has committed suicide, shooting himself... Before committing this act, he left the following message: "Who's the idiot who said there's no point in killing yourself, because you're always killing yourself too late?"
"Cioran," says fat Yelka, and she start to sing...

ROOM 214, PLEASE.

I GAVE YOU THE KEY FIVE MINUTES AGO, SIR, AND YOU WENT UP TO YOUR ROOM.

I DRAW MY EXXA 21... SO, MY DOUBLE'S ARRIVED. EVERYTHING MAKES SENSE, OF COURSE... EVEN MORE SO AS COBBEA STARTS WHISPERING IN MY SKULL AGAIN...

YOU HAVE TO ERADICATE THE FLY, HE SAYS. CRUSH IT WITH ONE BLOW, THE FIRST IF POSSIBLE... AND CONTINUE TO TRUST COBBEA, AS HE TRUSTS ME...

"GO," HE SAYS...

CONTROL THE ORIGINAL CAREFULLY. I WANT THIS TO GO QUICKLY.

...ORIGINAL SUBMISSIVE...

COME IN, NIKE... I WAS EXPECTING YOU...

HAPPY TO MEET YOU...

NOT AS HAPPY AS I AM...

IT'S REALLY NOT ADVISABLE TO SHOOT ONE'S DOUBLE, DEAR ORIGINAL...

COBBEA CONFIRMS THIS, **FORBIDDING ME TO SHOOT**.

THE CONNECTIONS FOR THE INITIALIZATION PROCESS HAVE BEEN ACTIVATED... STRIP TO THE WAIST, PLEASE...

I'M IN A HURRY.

A FLY BRUSHES BY MY EAR SOUNDING LIKE A GENERATOR... COBBEA ORDERS ME NOT TO TAKE MY EYES OFF IT... I'M THINKING OF AMIR. IF ONLY HE WERE HERE... EVEN ON D.3, THE FLY WOULDN'T HAVE A CHANCE WITH HIM...

AFRAID OF THE FLY?...

D.3... The sky is rumbling. Amir, newborn, sleeps... Nurses talk above our bed. The sniper who committed suicide is supposed to be his father... Someone by the name of Mladenovic, a Serb... But it's under the deceased mother's name, a Muslim, born Fazlagic, that his entry into the world has been registered... Amir, a two-day-old Muslim-Serb, has no parents but he's sleeping... And the sky is rumbling.

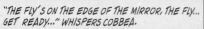

"THE FLY'S ON THE EDGE OF THE MIRROR, THE FLY... GET READY..." WHISPERS COBBEA.

THE INITIALIZATION ALLOWS ME TO PERFECT MY MEMORY CAPACITY AND THE SUBCUTANEOUS IMPLANT OF THE FLY WILL ONLY LAST LONG ENOUGH FOR IT TO LAY ITS SPY EGG...

"LAYING A SPY EGG?" I HARDLY HAVE TIME TO THINK THIS THROUGH WHEN COBBEA BEGINS SHOUTING INSIDE MY HEAD: "NOW!"

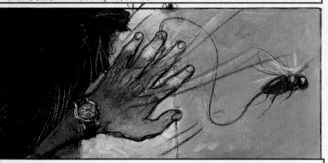

QUICK AS A FLASH I REACH OUT, BUT NOT EVERYONE IS AMIR... I MISS...

NEVER DO THAT AGAIN!

– FORTUNATELY, SPRINGING OUT OF MY SHAVING KIT WHERE HE'D MADE HIMSELF AT HOME, MINICAT DOESN'T MISS...

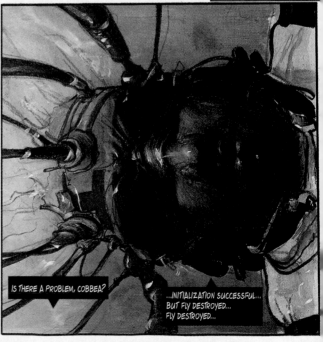

IS THERE A PROBLEM, COBBEA?

...INITIALIZATION SUCCESSFUL... BUT FLY DESTROYED... FLY DESTROYED...

ONE BROKEN NOSE AND DISMEMBERED FLY LATER...

GOOD WORK, MINICAT.

... WHILE THE DOUBLE SEEMS TO HAVE MOMENTARILY BLOWN SOME FUSES, COBBEA'S ORDERS START POURING INTO MY BRAIN. I SURPRISE MYSELF BY OBEYING THEM ALL, DOWN TO THE LAST DETAIL...

PULL OFF YOUR NOSE.
IT'S ALREADY DONE.

– EXTRACT THE METAL PLATE PLACED UNDER THE CARTILAGE OF YOUR NASAL PASSAGE.
– IT HURTS, BUT I'M DOING IT.

– STUFF THE PLATE INSIDE THE DOUBLE'S TORSO, ANYWHERE, AS DEEP AS POSSIBLE.

– DONE.

– BRAVO. NOW GET THE HELL OUT OF THE HOTEL. I'LL RE-CONTACT YOU. THANKS.

YOU'RE HIDING SOMETHING, COBBEA... WITHOUT A "SPY" IMPLANT I HAVE NO WITNESS, NO MORE CONTROL... WHAT HAPPENED?

...A PREDATOR...
FELINE...ACCIDENTAL...
UNFORESEEABLE...

... BUT SUCCESSFUL INITIALIZATION... AND THE DOUBLE IS REINITIALIZING ITS AUTONOMY...

I'LL BRING BACK THE DOUBLE AS PLANNED... BUT THE ORIGINAL... IS HE CAPABLE OF COMPLETING THE MISSION? PUT ANOTHER WAY, ARE YOU CAPABLE?

...I AM.

YOU'RE AWARE THAT I'M GOING TO STUFF YOU WITH ENOUGH "PRODUCTS" TO MAKE YOUR CORTEX IMPLODE?

...THAT IS WHAT I WANT. . . LET'S GET IT OVER WITH...

D.2... Here's Amir... Amir Fazlagic is born... I am one day older than him and I already know everything about the world into which he's arriving, in which we're...

I'm thinking of Leyla, who is going to join us in a week (or who "left" us a week ago, by my memory's countdown)... So we are (will be) three in this bed... Pure, perfect orphans... Without parents since our very first day... I remember crying about it silently while looking into Amir's eyes... Amir who didn't see me, who was howling for no apparent reason, as newborns do...

Above our heads, through the hole in the hospital, the sky is blue...

A FEW DAYS AFTER SARAJEVO AND AFTER VARIOUS STOPOVERS ARRANGED BY COBBEA: LIMASOL (CHARMING), ALEXANDRIA (MAGICAL), AMMAN (CROWDED), BAYIR (STRANGE), I FIND MYSELF IN A CAB IN THE MIDDLE OF THE NEFOUD DESERT, DESTINATION LEYLA... WHAT I LIVED THROUGH FACING MY DOUBLE WILL QUICKLY BECOME A PART OF THE FEW, BUT SPECTACULAR, HOLES IN MY INFALLIBLE MEMORY...

THEY SAY HE'S JUST HAD AN ELEVATOR INSTALLED SO HE CAN GO UP TO THE STARS... BUT OTHER THAN HIS DAUGHTER, OLD ZOHARY NEVER HAS VISITORS...

ARE YOU FAMILY?

IN A WAY...

COBBEA MAKES A BRIEF INCURSION IN MY HEAD AS THE SHADOW OF A SHADOW... HIS VOICE, ITS CONCISION AND ITS WEAK SIGNAL, SEEMS TO REVEAL A PROFOUND SUFFERING... IN TELEGRAPH STYLE, HE SAYS: ...DOUBLE IS BACK, STOP.. WELL PLAYED ONCE AGAIN, STOP.. I'VE HAD IT, STOP.. WILL TRY ONE LAST BLUFF, STOP.. PAMELA FISHER, ESCAPE, STOP.. THIS MY LAST MESSAGE, STOP... FAREWELL, STOP

OLD ZOHARY WAS A GREAT ASTRONOMER, BUT ALSO A GREAT POLITICIAN... ONE OF THE LAST HUMANISTS...

ISN'T YOUR CAB MAKING A STRANGE NOISE?

YOU'VE HEARD LIEUTENANT COBBEA, GENTLEMEN. IT WOULD SEEM THAT "MY" CHOSEN ONE HAS REACHED THE FAMOUS EAGLE SITE...

IT WOULD ONLY "SEEM?" AREN'T YOU SURE OF IT?

I TRUST MY SYSTEM, EVEN THOUGH THERE IS NO WAY TO VERIFY THAT "MY" COBBEA IS CORRECT... HOWEVER, I'M ALWAYS READY TO GAMBLE, SO I'M READY TO UNLEASH THE FIRE OF THE SKY WHENEVER YOU WISH... AT THE VERY WORST, IT'LL BE A WASTED SHOT INTO A STRETCH OF SAND... ALL I HAVE TO DO IS PRESS A BUTTON AND THE ORDER WILL BE TRANSMITTED TO AN AIRBORNE OPTICAL SYSTEM THAT INSTANTLY ACTIVATES THE LASER SATELLITE. IT IS ALREADY LOCKED ONTO ITS TARGET – THE CHOSEN ONE'S NOSE. THE IMPACT WILL TAKE PLACE IN SEVEN MINUTES...

BUT I COULD ALSO CANCEL THE WHOLE OPERATION. IT'S YOUR CALL, GENTLEMEN...

WE'RE OFF.. I DON'T KNOW TO WHERE, BUT WE'RE OFF..

THE VEHICLE IS SET FOR A MEDIUM DISTANCE, SOMEWHERE IN THE EAST.

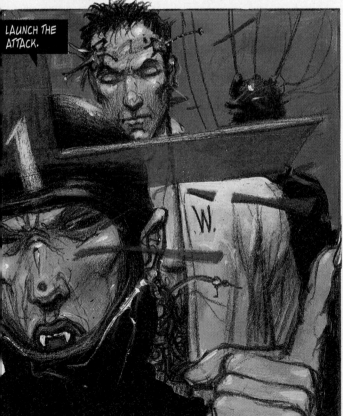

LAUNCH THE ATTACK.

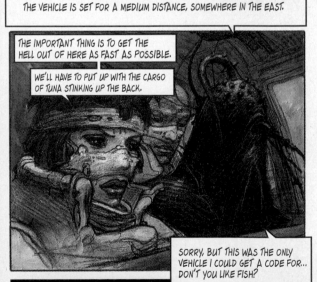

THE IMPORTANT THING IS TO GET THE HELL OUT OF HERE AS FAST AS POSSIBLE.

WE'LL HAVE TO PUT UP WITH THE CARGO OF TUNA STINKING UP THE BACK.

SORRY, BUT THIS WAS THE ONLY VEHICLE I COULD GET A CODE FOR... DON'T YOU LIKE FISH?

I arrive at the hospital on D.2, barely two days old... I remember... The doctor, whose first name is Berzad, examines me. He turns me over and over in every direction. I throw up everything I've never eaten...

IT'S MAGNIFICENT, LEYLA... I'M AT 33,000 METERS AND IT'S STILL CLIMBING!

Earlier the same day, I hear that my father is dead. He was shot in the forehead by the most resourceful and twisted sniper in Sarajevo. My father had no papers on him and was unknown in the city... He wore "Nike" sneakers... The journalist who found me is called Hatzfeld and this fucking war is about to awaken the Beast.

I CAN SEE AN ENORMOUS SHOOTING STAR I THE ATMOSPHER TO THE NORTH- EAST, AROUND SIBERIA... A METEORITE... OR MAYBE A LASER BEAM...

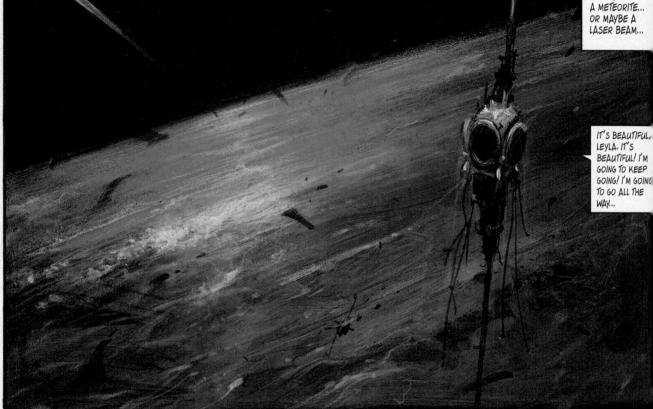

IT'S BEAUTIFUL, LEYLA. IT'S BEAUTIFUL! I'M GOING TO KEEP GOING! I'M GOING TO GO ALL THE WAY...

IMPACT IN FEWER THAN THREE MINUTES, GENTLEMEN...

WARHOLE... FUCKING WARHOLE, CAN YOU HEAR ME...?

I DIDN'T KNOW YOU COULD BE SO VULGAR, LIEUTENANT.

WHAT DOES THIS MEAN?

IF THAT'S THE CASE, I'D SAY YOU'RE VERY GOOD, LIEUTENANT, AND I CONGRATULATE YOU. . .

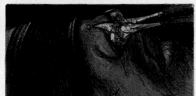

ABOUT THE IMPACT, WHAT WOULD YOU SAY IF I WERE TO TELL YOU THAT THE REAL NIKE HATZFELD'S NOSE IS IN THE TORSO OF THE FAKE ONE, YOU FUCKER?

I REPEAT, WHAT DOES THIS MEAN?

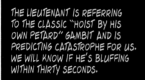

THE LIEUTENANT IS REFERRING TO THE CLASSIC "HOIST BY HIS OWN PETARD" GAMBIT AND IS PREDICTING CATASTROPHE FOR US. WE WILL KNOW IF HE'S BLUFFING WITHIN THIRTY SECONDS.

DIE, ALL OF YOU! FUCK YOU ALL!

IN THE EVENT THAT THE LIEUTENANT IS TELLING THE TRUTH AND IN CONSIDERATION OF THE LAST FIFTEEN SECONDS WE HAVE LEFT...

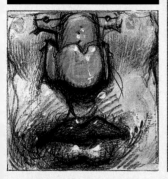

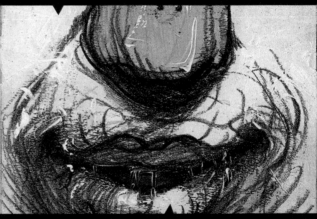

I FEEL OBLIGED TO TELL YOU THAT THE WARHOLE YOU HAVE BEFORE YOU IS NOT, OF COURSE, THE ORIGINAL...

FAREWELL, GENTLEMEN... FIVE SECONDS, FOUR, THREE, TWO...

I FEEL A SWITCH BEING FLIPPED IN MY BRAIN AND INSTANTLY REALIZE THAT COBBEA, ON THE OTHER SIDE OF THE WORLD, HAS WON HIS BET AND HE'S DEAD AS A RESULT... THE CONTACT'S BEEN CUT AND I FEEL, IF I MAY SAY SO, EVEN MORE OF AN ORPHAN...
I THINK OF HIM...

COBBEA...

Still D.2... It's taken the shape of an obsessive litany that I can't get away from... My father was killed by Amir's... My father was killed by Amir's... My father was killed by Amir's...

IT LOOKS LIKE MY FIVE HOURS OF WALKING ARE GOING TO BE HARD...

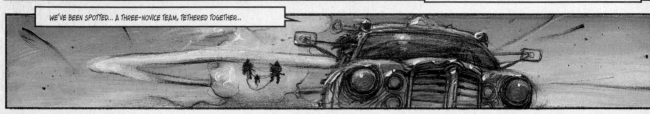

WE'VE BEEN SPOTTED... A THREE-NOVICE TEAM, TETHERED TOGETHER...

NOVICES?

DO WE HAVE ANY WEAPONS?

SOME VEHICLES ARE EQUIPPED AND PROGRAMMED TO RESPOND IN THE EVENT OF AN ATTACK... WE'RE GOING TO FIND OUT VERY QUICKLY.

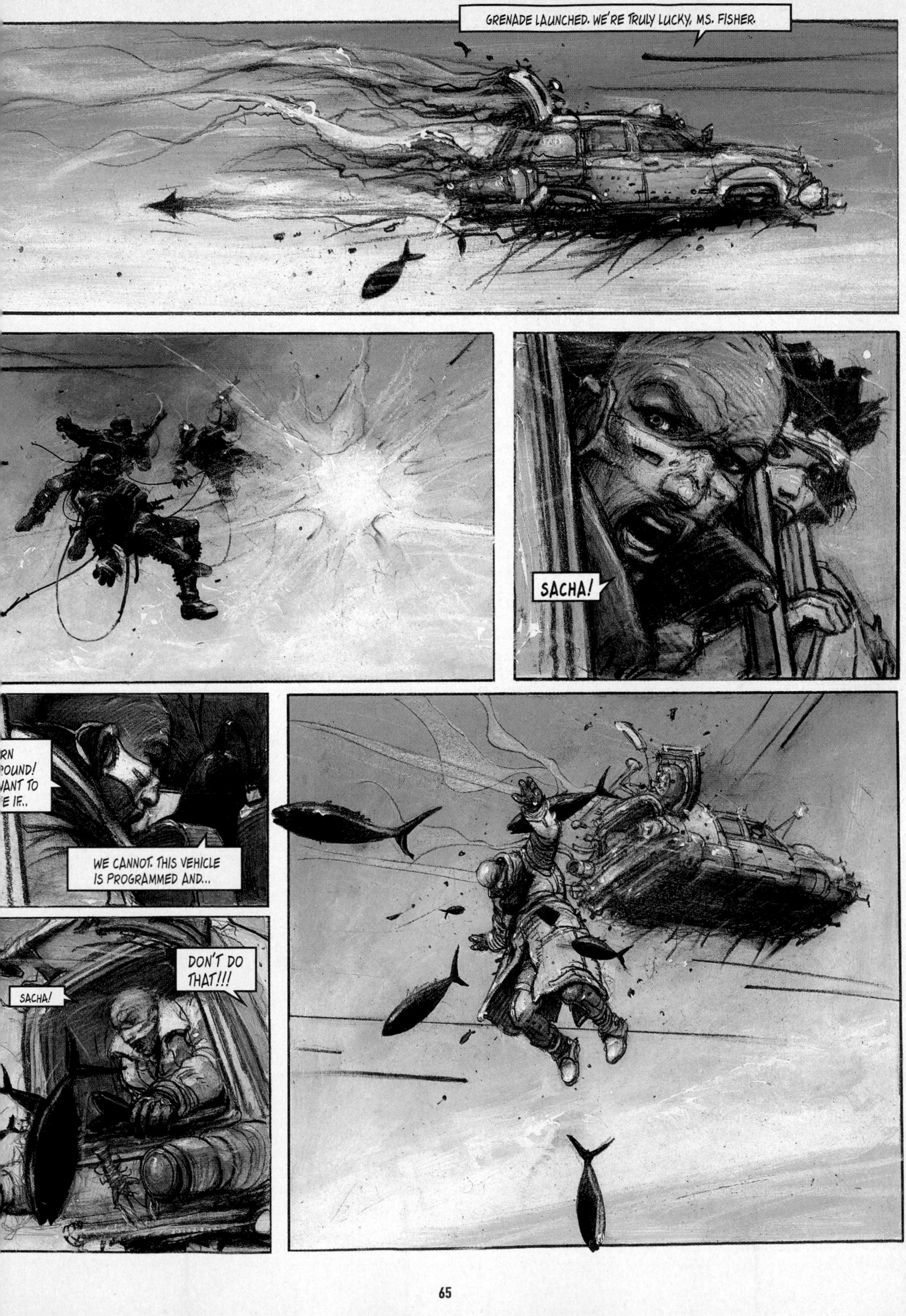
GRENADE LAUNCHED. WE'RE TRULY LUCKY, MS. FISHER.
SACHA!
WE CANNOT. THIS VEHICLE IS PROGRAMMED AND...
DON'T DO THAT!!!
SACHA!

HELLO, I'M LOOKING FOR LEYLA MIRKOVIC-ZOHARY... IS THAT YOU?

...AND YOU, YOU'RE NIKE HATZFELD... YOU'RE THE ONE WHO CALLED...

ARE YOU OKAY?

YOU CAME AT A BAD TIME... I'M IN THE MIDDLE OF LOSING MY FATHER...

SORRY...

IS HE SERI- OUSLY ILL?

NO, HE'S SERIOUS HAPPY.

D.1... I've got light in my eyes. I can't see anything. I remember, I can't see a thing... But I hear sounds, violent ones. Some are mechanical, the sound of bombs, other are organic, the cries of men... The two combined conjugate death. I learn this on Day One, a day of blind shelling, the day of my birth...
I also hear a voice, it is the sweetest voice, which talks to me, talks to me, but which drifts away, drifts away... Have I been snatched away from this voice, or has it been snatched away from me? The one running and carrying me is my father, the one I will never hear again was my mother... A gunshot in Sniper Alley and everything goes...

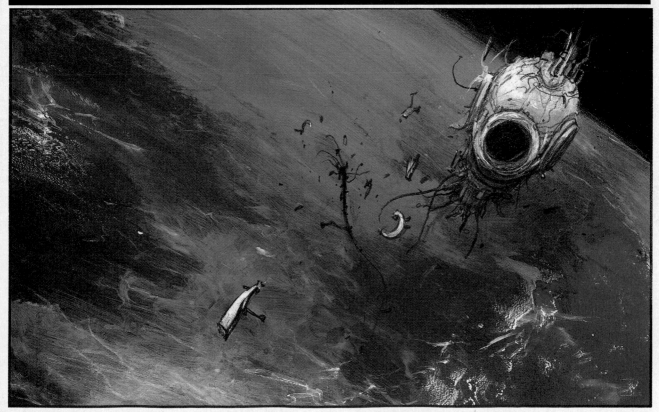

I REMEMBER... I'M EIGHTEEN DAYS OLD AND I REMEMBER THE HUGE BLACK FLIES AND THE TEPID SUMMER AIR SINKING IN THROUGH THE GAPING HOLES IN THE HOSPITAL. EIGHTEEN DAYS OLD AND I CAN ALREADY TELL THE DIFFERENCE BETWEEN A BLAST OF AIR AND THE BLASTING OF BOMBS, BETWEEN AN EXPLODING MORTAR AND AN EXPLODING T34... EIGHTEEN DAYS OLD AND I KNOW THAT I'M AN ORPHAN AND THAT MY NAME IS NIKE... TO MY LEFT IN THE SAME BED SLEEPS AMIR, A DAY YOUNGER THAN I AM AND TO MY RIGHT, LEYLA, THE YOUNGEST, BARELY TEN DAYS OLD, IS CRYING... THEY TOO ARE ORPHANS, BUT THEY DON'T KNOW IT. I'M THE OLDEST AND I SWEAR BY THE STARS THAT SHINE OVERHEAD, HIGH ABOVE THE ROOF THAT'S BEEN BLOWN AWAY, THAT I'LL PROTECT THEM FOREVER...

SHE USED TO SAY, "AMIR, DO YOU LOVE ME? DO YOU LOVE ME?"

THEN SHE'D REPEAT IT THREE TIMES: "DO YOU LOVE ME? DO YOU LOVE ME? DO YOU LOVE ME?..."

AND I'D ASK HER RIGHT BACK, "AND YOU, SACHA? DO YOU LOVE ME?"

AND SHE'D SAY IT THREE TIMES: "I LOVE YOU, I LOVE YOU, I LOVE YOU..."

"FLY... TUNA... IT ALL MAKES SENSE... AN EROTIC NIGHTMARE. IT'S ALMOST BORING CONSIDERING WHAT ACTUALLY HAPPENED ..."

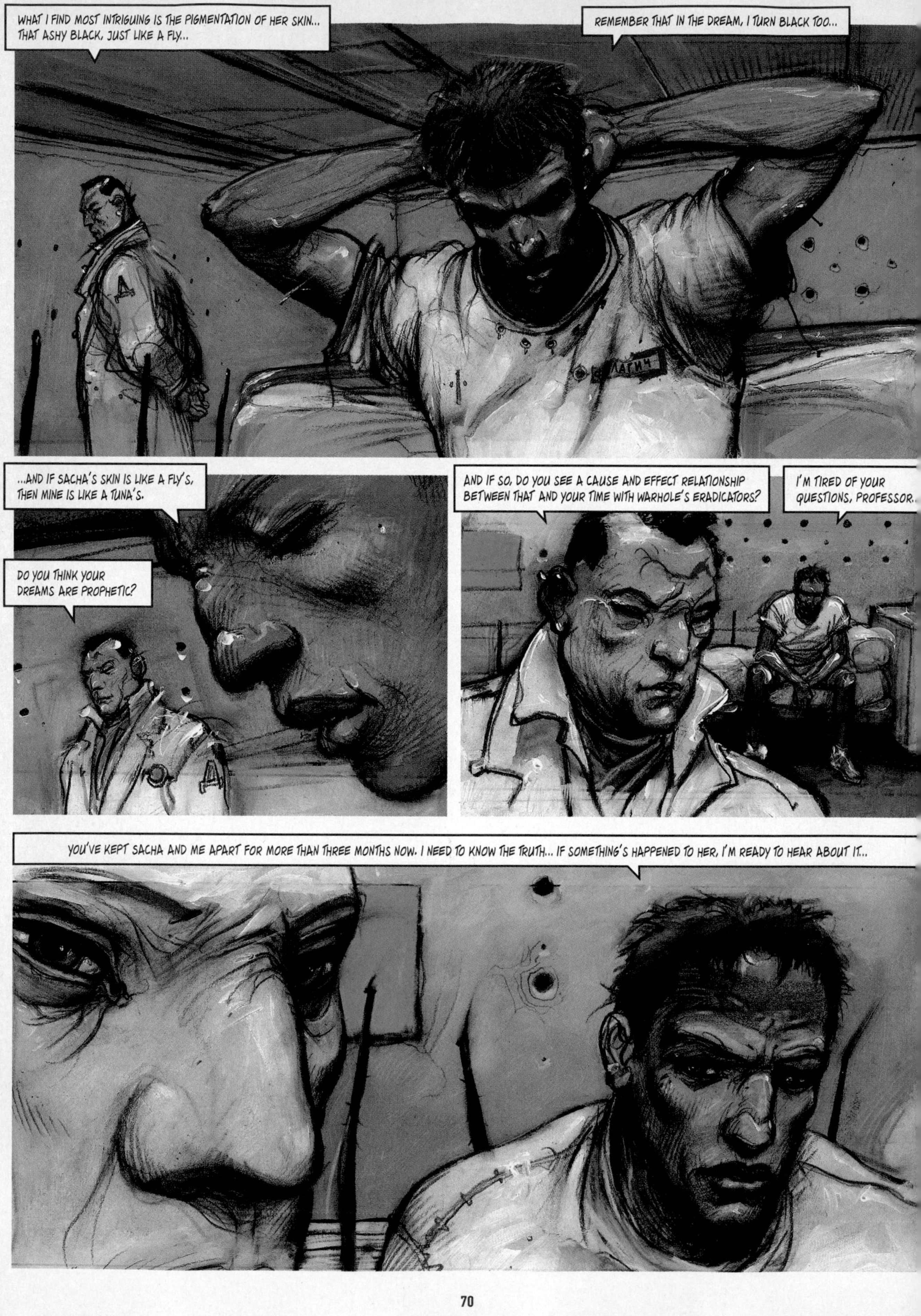
WHAT I FIND MOST INTRIGUING IS THE PIGMENTATION OF HER SKIN... THAT ASHY BLACK, JUST LIKE A FLY...
REMEMBER THAT IN THE DREAM, I TURN BLACK TOO...
...AND IF SACHA'S SKIN IS LIKE A FLY'S, THEN MINE IS LIKE A TUNA'S.
DO YOU THINK YOUR DREAMS ARE PROPHETIC?
AND IF SO, DO YOU SEE A CAUSE AND EFFECT RELATIONSHIP BETWEEN THAT AND YOUR TIME WITH WARHOLE'S ERADICATORS?
I'M TIRED OF YOUR QUESTIONS, PROFESSOR.
YOU'VE KEPT SACHA AND ME APART FOR MORE THAN THREE MONTHS NOW. I NEED TO KNOW THE TRUTH... IF SOMETHING'S HAPPENED TO HER, I'M READY TO HEAR ABOUT IT...

Rinat Gazzaev, Islamic scientific officer from the Irkoutsk province, was as stubborn as I am, but he was a good man.

Sacha and I owe him for helping us escape from the more radical Russian and international wings after the destruction of Optus Warhole's Eradicator camp and for our unexpected rescue (thanks to a certain Pamela Fisher) in the frozen Siberian desert...

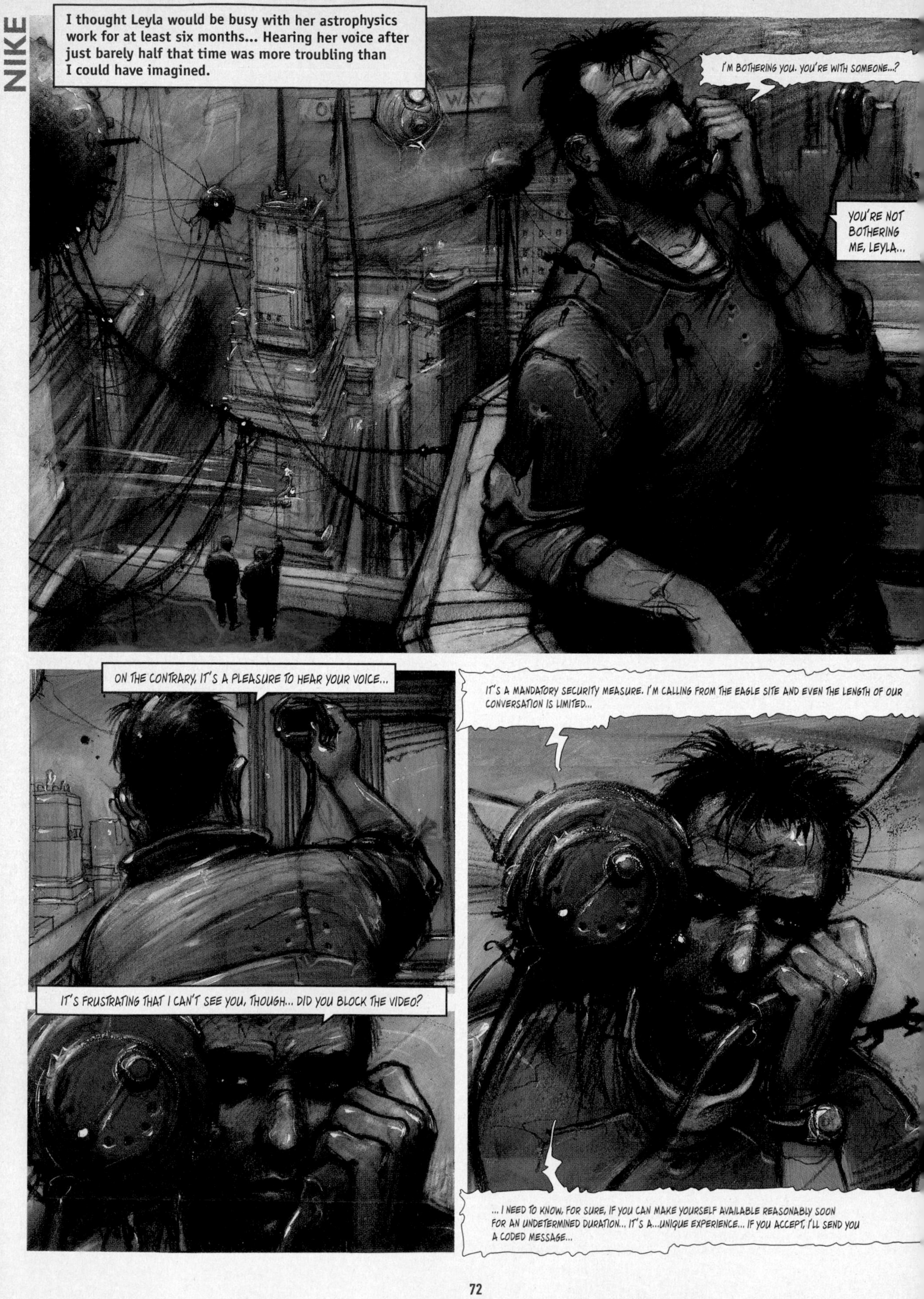
NIKE
I thought Leyla would be busy with her astrophysics work for at least six months... Hearing her voice after just barely half that time was more troubling than I could have imagined.
I'M BOTHERING YOU. YOU'RE WITH SOMEONE...?
YOU'RE NOT BOTHERING ME, LEYLA...
ON THE CONTRARY, IT'S A PLEASURE TO HEAR YOUR VOICE...
IT'S FRUSTRATING THAT I CAN'T SEE YOU, THOUGH... DID YOU BLOCK THE VIDEO?
IT'S A MANDATORY SECURITY MEASURE. I'M CALLING FROM THE EAGLE SITE AND EVEN THE LENGTH OF OUR CONVERSATION IS LIMITED...
... I NEED TO KNOW, FOR SURE, IF YOU CAN MAKE YOURSELF AVAILABLE REASONABLY SOON FOR AN UNDETERMINED DURATION... IT'S A...UNIQUE EXPERIENCE... IF YOU ACCEPT, I'LL SEND YOU A CODED MESSAGE...

WHEN DO YOU WANT AN ANSWER?

NOW...

...OTHERWISE I'LL CHOOSE SOMEONE ELSE.

I'M STILL NOT SO GOOD AT MAKING SNAP DECISIONS...

DON'T YOU WANT TO SEE ME SOONER RATHER THAN LATER? I CUT MY HAIR...

NIKE?... DID YOU HEAR ME? YES OR NO?

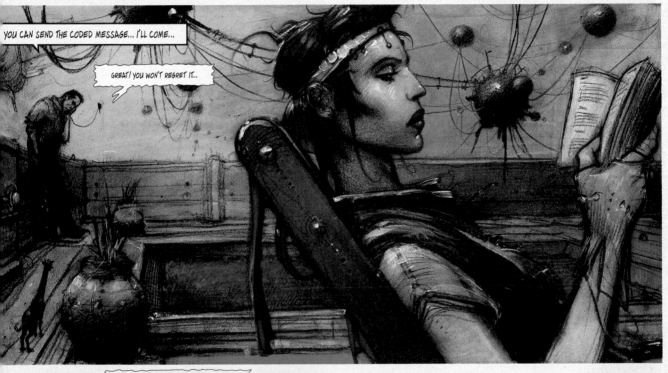

YOU CAN SEND THE CODED MESSAGE... I'LL COME...

GREAT! YOU WON'T REGRET IT...

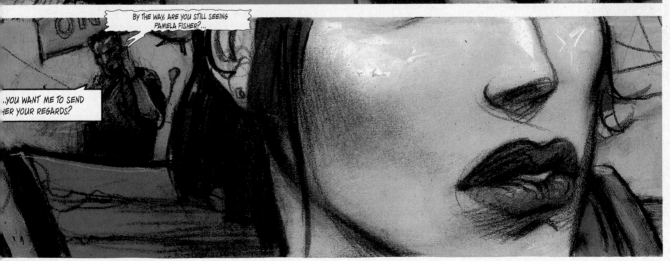

BY THE WAY, ARE YOU STILL SEEING PAMELA FISHER?...

..YOU WANT ME TO SEND HER YOUR REGARDS?

LEYLA

I don't like Pamela Fisher. I don't know her and I don't like her. I imagine her as a reptile, always the same temperature. Jealousy, pure and simple, I admit it. But that's just how it is.

Ever since I met Nike, in this very desert, six months ago, not a day has gone by, not an hour (a second?), despite the richness of my work on the Eagle Site, that I haven't thought of him, of Amir, who has vanished, of our "three-part story." His arrival in my life, on the very day that my father was leaving it forever, is a constant, deep, endless turmoil, just like his memory... Nike was the engraver of my first moments of life. My big brother, ten days older than me, he gave me what was left of Sarajevo, he gave me secrets I could never have known otherwise... He is the historian of my birth.
But this is what I both know and fear: Nike is much more than that... I don't like not liking her, but I do not like Pamela Fisher... It's going to be too hot tomorrow.

SORRY TO INTERRUPT YOUR DAYDREAMING, LEYLA, BUT I HAVE IMPORTANT NEWS. THE DALAÏ LAMA IS COMING. NOW WE JUST NEED THE POPE TO CONFIRM, BUT HE REALLY DOESN'T HAVE A CHOICE ANYMORE.

NIKE HATZFELD IS COMING TOO.

NIKE

LEYLA SENDS HER BEST...

HOW NICE OF HER...

WHILE WE'RE ON THE SUBJECT, I HAVE SOMETHING TO SAY... AND I HAVE A QUESTION...

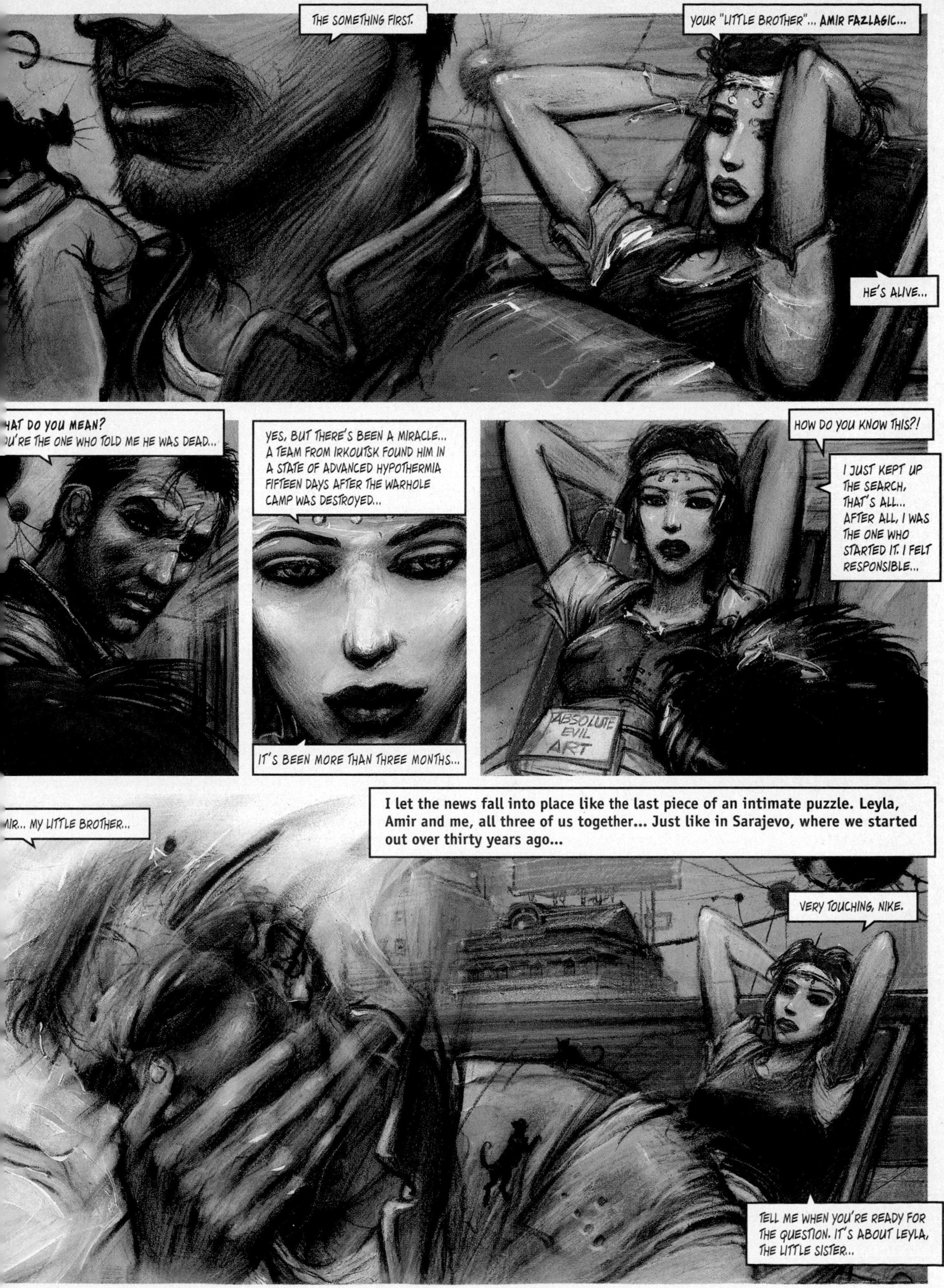
THE SOMETHING FIRST.
YOUR "LITTLE BROTHER"... AMIR FAZLAGIC...
HE'S ALIVE...
HAT DO YOU MEAN?
U'RE THE ONE WHO TOLD ME HE WAS DEAD...
YES, BUT THERE'S BEEN A MIRACLE... A TEAM FROM IRKOUTSK FOUND HIM IN A STATE OF ADVANCED HYPOTHERMIA FIFTEEN DAYS AFTER THE WARHOLE CAMP WAS DESTROYED...
IT'S BEEN MORE THAN THREE MONTHS...
HOW DO YOU KNOW THIS?!
I JUST KEPT UP THE SEARCH, THAT'S ALL... AFTER ALL, I WAS THE ONE WHO STARTED IT. I FELT RESPONSIBLE...
ABSOLUTE EVIL ART
IR... MY LITTLE BROTHER...
I let the news fall into place like the last piece of an intimate puzzle. Leyla, Amir and me, all three of us together... Just like in Sarajevo, where we started out over thirty years ago...
VERY TOUCHING, NIKE.
TELL ME WHEN YOU'RE READY FOR THE QUESTION. IT'S ABOUT LEYLA, THE LITTLE SISTER...

In the fraction of a second that follows this question I hesitate between two answers:
"Would you sleep with your little brother?" and "A guy doesn't sleep with his little sister, you know?"

...But mostly I feel reassured because Pamela's excessive jealousy feels to me like evidence that she is human... Images of the attack at the "Water-Shop" in New York (it's been a year) and of the gnarled torso of her android double dripping synthetic body fluids are still burned into my brain...that explosion was the beginning of a terrifying story.

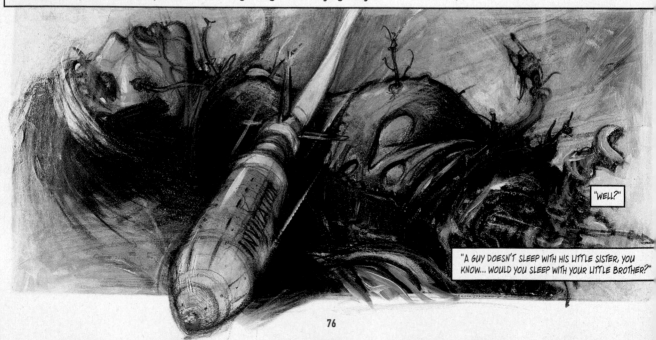

If a mini atom bomb had detonated at our feet, or a splinter of the deck had pulverized my nose (for the third time in a year...), anything in that extremely violent time would have whispered a warning in my ear (already blown out by the explosion). ANYTHING would have been better than an INVITATION. Because that's how it all started up again.

IT'S NO BIG DEAL, NIKE. JUST AN INVITATION...

I'M TOUCHED, THANKS...

THE EXPLOSION IS HARMLESS, I PROMISE!

IT'S NUCLEAR LIGHT. THE WORDS WILL WRITE THEMSELVES IN THE CONCRETE... LOOK, THE TEXT IS APPEARING... IT'S STRAIGHT FROM JEFFER... HE'S A GENIUS!

WHAT ARE YOU TALKING ABOUT?

JEFFER... JEFFERSON HOLERAW! A DEAR FRIEND. HE'S INVITING US TO A P.P. (PRIVATE PARTY)... HE'S A V.G.A. (VERY GREAT ARTIST)...

"Holeraw? I've never heard of him..." must have been my stupid response.

I THINK THE IDEA OF NEO-NUCLEAR POWER AS ART IS GREAT STUFF THIS INVITATION IS AN ACT OF PURE CREATION IN ITSELF... I'M DISAPPOINTED THAT YOU DON'T APPRECIATE IT...

Pamela had been back in my life for barely two weeks... I was letting her stay at my place while she got over her fears and the trauma of Optus Warhole's Siberian Obscurantist hell and while my own memory recovered from its dizzying and painful performance.

We had decided not to renew our love affair (the only sexual contact that she'd imposed on me when she got there was meant to prove that she was indeed the "real" Pamela Fisher).
To fight my huge paranoia and the sorry results of the whole experience, she blindfolded me and made me lick a drop of her blood and then one of my own. But the thickness of the liquid of one and the too-pronounced taste of iron in the other only made me more uncertain.

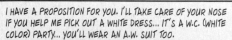

I HAVE A PROPOSITION FOR YOU. I'LL TAKE CARE OF YOUR NOSE IF YOU HELP ME PICK OUT A WHITE DRESS... IT'S A W.C. (WHITE COLOR) PARTY... YOU'LL WEAR AN A.W. SUIT TOO.

...DEPARTURE IN 48 HOURS... DESTINATION: HOLERAW BUILDING, BANGKOK...

A.W. ?

YES, ALL WHITE...

Why did I accept those orders, delivered in the firm and assured voice (a synthetic remix?) of Pamela Fisher?

ARE WE LEAVING IRKOUTSK?

SACHA IS OUTSIDE THE CITY. I MOVE HER AROUND FREQUENTLY.

MORE AND MORE PEOPLE SEEM TO BE INTERESTED IN HER CASE. OF COURSE, I TRY TO SHIELD HER FROM ALL OF THAT...

WHAT KIND OF PEOPLE?

PEOPLE IN SCIENCE, IN POWER, IN COMMUNICATION, IN ECONOMICS AND MAFIA MONEY, THE RELIGIOUS POWERS AND THEIR FOLLOWERS... PEOPLE FROM ALL OVER THE WORLD.

RIGHT. THE POWERS THAT BE...

YOU'RE VERY NAÏVE, YOUNG MAN... BUT YOU'LL CHANGE YOUR MIND WHEN YOU SEE HER...

79

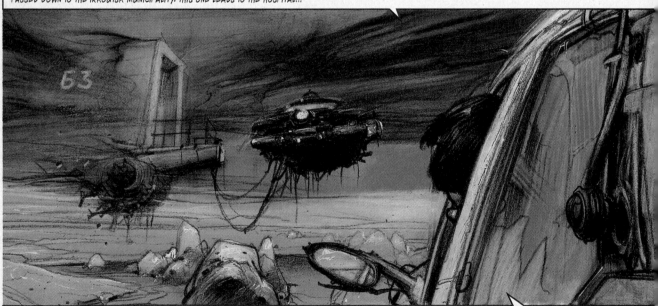

These "entryways" date from the last Sino-Russo-Mongol conflict... They were also used to fight against the obscurantist order... A few of them have been passed down to the Irkoutsk municipality. This one leads to the hospital...

The doors are useful because they keep people away. This whole zone stretching out to the east is linked to the war, to death. People are afraid to enter...

THE "TRANSFER" WILL BE SEAMLESS. WE'LL MOVE INSTANTLY INTO THE PARALLEL DIMENSION. IT'S NOT VERY GOOD FOR THE BODY BUT YOU WON'T FEEL A THING.

I didn't feel anything. I didn't see anything. But there was the smell.
The smell of blood.
Then just one thought: Sacha.
Where is Sacha?!
Her name flew from my mouth in an uncontrolled cry as long as the endless virtual corridor.

"Amir," came the answer, it was her voice, crying out as well.

Then there was a sob. "Don't look at me!"

SACHA...

Then pleading.

DON'T LOOK AT ME...

I held her body tight. She had anthracite skin right out of my nightmares. I held her tight for a long time. As if to say "Of course it doesn't change a thing, of course I'll still love you, even like this, especially like this, even more than before if that's possible and besides, I like the dark skin, it looks good on you, it makes you even more beautiful than before if that's possible and maybe, if it's possible to change it, you shouldn't, because why go back to the way it was before when you look so good like this..."

...ESPECIALLY WITH YOUR GREEN EYES... EYES THAT I WANT TO SEE WITHOUT THESE TEARS IN THEM...

It was because I was scared and because I didn't want Sacha to see it that all these words came tumbling out of my mouth. But the more I talked, the tighter I held her and the more the trembling in my legs betrayed me.

WHAT HAPPENED, MISS KRYLOVA?

EXACTLY WHAT YOU WERE AFRAID OF. THOSE TWO MEN CAME, THEY SHOT THE NURSE AND I SHOT THEM WITH THE GUN YOU GAVE ME... I DIDN'T THINK IT WOULD TEAR THEM TO SHREDS...

ME NEITHER...

YOU ARM YOUR PATIENTS NOW, PROFESSOR?

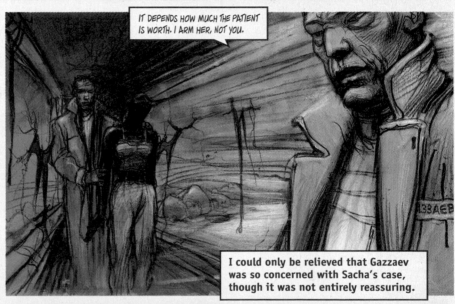

IT DEPENDS HOW MUCH THE PATIENT IS WORTH. I ARM HER, NOT YOU.

I could only be relieved that Gazzaev was so concerned with Sacha's case, though it was not entirely reassuring.

WE'RE GOING TO HAVE TO LEAVE THIS PORT AND GO TO ANOTHER... THE THREE OF US TOGETHER.

I've heard that before.

The Dalaï Lama turned out to be an easy collaborator, canny and zen as you'd expect, even though he found the levitating chair a little dilapidated for his tastes. His descent into the heart of the site, accompanied by a guard, went smoothly. He told me that the Pope would be arriving any minute, but I just wanted to see Nike.

NIKE

"JEFFERSON HOLERAW SPEAKING. WELCOME TO THE EXPRESS ELEVATOR TO THE 67TH FLOOR, THE APEX OF THIS HUMBLE BUILDING. IT SEEMS THAT NOT EVERYONE FOLLOWED MY INSTRUCTIONS FOR THE "ALL WHITE THEME" TO THE LETTER. THEREFORE, PLEASE CLOSE YOUR EYES AND MOUTHS FOR A LITTLE VAPORIZATION RETOUCH... ENJOY THE RIDE. I'M WAITING FOR YOU UPSTAIRS."

IS IT PAINT?

YOU COULD SAY THAT...

THIS WAY, WE'RE ALL SURE TO BE WHITE AND RIDICULOUS... I GUESS IT'S HARMLESS... LIKE THE NUCLEAR BOMB INVITATION BACK IN NEW YORK...

YOU DON'T MISS A THING.

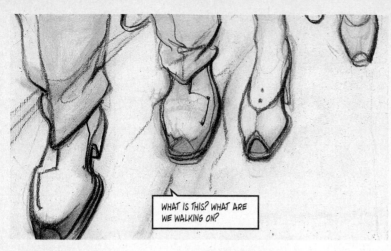

WHAT IS THIS? WHAT ARE WE WALKING ON?

ON CANVAS, WHITE CANVAS... THE WALLS AND THE CEILING ARE COVERED IN IT TOO...

IT'S PRETTY.

NIKE, LET ME INTRODUCE YOU TO MY FRIEND MILORAD ZIVKOVIC ...

NIKE HATZFELD, I PRESUME...

YOU PRESUME CORRECTLY.

WOULD YOU BELIEVE THAT OUR PATHS HAVE CROSSED ONCE BEFORE...? IT WAS A LITTLE MORE THAN THIRTY-THREE YEARS AGO, IN SARAJEVO... YOU WERE ONE DAY OLD... I KNOW YOU HAVE THE ABILITY TO REMEMBER THAT FAR BACK...

I'LL SEE YOU LATER...

HOW ABOUT WE GO HAVE A GLASS OF SLJIVOVICA ON THE BALCONY... A REUNION LIKE THIS IS CAUSE FOR CELEBRATION.

Right away I knew something was up with this guy. Aggression flowed from his every pore. I told myself that Pamela had some strange friends and that I should just stay calm.

LET'S DRINK TO YOUR FRIEND AMIR FAZLAGIC AND HIS MIRACULOUS RECOVERY...

THE STORY OF YOUR TRIAD IS PRETTY TOUCHING, BY THE WAY, YOU TWO AND LITTLE LEYLA...

YOU KNOW A LOT ABOUT ME.

...TOO BAD THE LITTLE ASSHOLE TOOK HIS WHORE OF A MUSLIM MOTHER'S NAME... FAZLAGIC, SOUNDS AS DIRTY AS A TURK, DOESN'T IT?

Calm, stay calm...

HIS FATHER'S NAME SOUNDED BETTER... IT SOUNDED SERBIAN... MLADENOVIC! HIS FATHER WAS MY BEST FRIEND...

How could he know all this? Pamela? Impossible... Though it might be, if...

WE WERE BOTH BIATHLON CHAMPIONS. SKILLED SKIERS AND GREAT SHOTS...

Got to stay calm. Get a little of the 90-proof plum alcohol in your mouth and hold it there. Let it burn your palate, so you know you're not dreaming.

"ONCE WE BECAME SNIPERS, WE WERE INSEPARABLE... WE CHANGED BUILDINGS EVERY DAY. WE LOVED EACH OTHER. WE SHOT AT EVERYTHING THAT PASSED... THE FUNNY THING, YOU'LL BE INTERESTED IN THIS, WAS THAT WE MADE A BET WHEN WE SAW YOUR FATHER COME OUTSIDE WAY DOWN ON LJUBLJANSKA STREET. IT WAS REALLY FAR, AT THE VERY EDGE OF OUR GUNS' RANGE. THAT BASTARD GOT HIM. AS HE FELL, YOUR FATHER DROPPED SOMETHING... IF I'D ONLY KNOWN IT WAS YOU... BUT THAT'S LIFE, RIGHT, NIKE HATZFELD?... AND THEN WE WOULDN'T HAVE HAD THE PLEASURE OF SHARING A DRINK TONIGHT..."

As calm as possible... Wait it out.

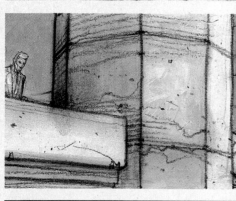

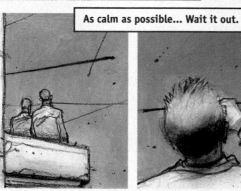

WE WERE CAUGHT THAT VERY DAY. THOSE SHITS OF BOSNIAN MUSLIMS FOUND US, PUT THEIR MOUDHAHIDIN GUNS TO OUR BACKS. WE MANAGED TO ESCAPE. A FEW DAYS LATER, MLADENOVIC'S WIFE DIED IN CHILDBIRTH AND HE SHOT HIMSELF. HE WAS HIS OWN LAST SNIPER VICTIM. THE TWENTY-SECOND.

ANOTHER GLASS OF SLJIVOVICA?

The punch was graceful and simple. Elegance itself. A calm and precise punch.

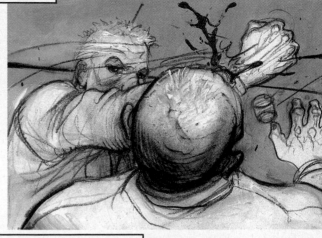

He soared sixty-seven stories...

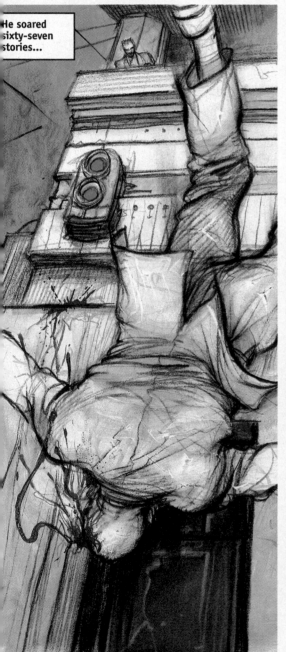

...Just as Pamela was coming back.

NIKE, I'D LIKE YOU TO MEET JEFFERSON HOLERAW.

THAT WAS QUITE A GESTURE. HE MUST HAVE CRACKED HIS SKULL ON THE RAIL OF THE WHITE MARBLE TERRACE SIX FLOORS DOWN BEFORE HITTING THE CEMENT TWO HUNDRED AND THIRTY METERS LOWER... A SUBLIME POINT OF RED IN ALL THAT WHITE! THANK YOU SO MUCH FOR STARTING OFF TONIGHT'S HAPPENING.

Then one hundred and seventy-four hands, belonging to eighty-seven people, began to applaud me.

BRAVO, NIKE! YOU SEE, IT'S ALL GOING SO WELL...

I was among madmen.

I'M WORRIED ABOUT THIS CROWD'S SANITY, PAMELA AND ABOUT YOURS TOO.

YOU JUST NEED TO GET USED TO IT.

RIGHT NOW I NEED A LAWYER. IN CASE YOU DIDN'T NOTICE, I JUST COMMITTED MURDER.

EXACTLY. THE FIRST BRUSH-STROKE ON A VIRGIN CANVAS IS ALWAYS THE MOST IMPORTANT. THAT'S WHAT THAT MURDER WAS, DON'T YOU SEE?

LOOK! THERE'S THE SECOND...

And the brushstrokes began falling all around me.

Cheerful splashes of red were covering the white canvas of the Very Great Artist named Holeraw. Blood spurted from a throat cut here, a vein sliced there (so there were even suicides!) and who knows what other fatal wounds. "Isn't it beautiful?!" cried Pamela, a bloody knife in her hand, on her knees in front of a massacred young woman. "An old rival," she explained.

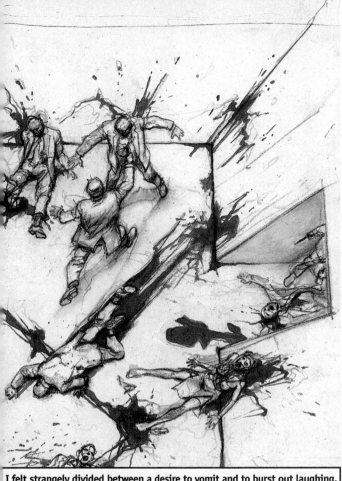

I felt strangely divided between a desire to vomit and to burst out laughing.

ended up doing both at once in a sink.

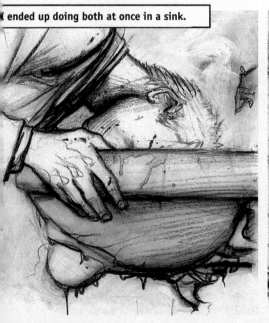

SO, NIKE HATZFELD HAS A DELICATE STOMACH?

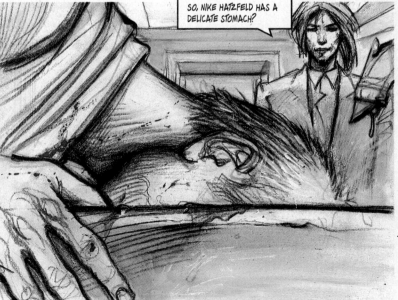

My mouth was still too full to answer. And what would I have said, anyway?

LET ME FILL YOU IN. THERE ARE NO TRUE HUMANS INVOLVED IN THIS CARNAGE. THESE ARE ALL PERFECT REPLICAS. THE BLOOD YOU SEE IS HALF SYNTHETIC, EVEN IF IT DOES HAVE THE RIGHT TASTE AND COLOR. PAMELA IS NOT THE REAL PAMELA AND I MYSELF AM PERFECTLY ARTIFICIAL AND NON-HUMAN...

WHAT ARE YOU TALKING ABOUT?

AND YOU, DON'T BE SO SURE YOU'RE THE REAL NIKE HATZFELD.

WHAT ARE YOU TALKING ABOUT?!!!

CALM DOWN. I HAVE NO DOUBT THAT YOUR ENORMOUS INTELLECTUAL CAPABILITIES HAVE HELPED YOU DEDUCE THE SIMPLE ANAGRAM HIDING BEHIND THE NAME HOLERAW...

AM I MISTAKEN?

He was mistaken, obviously. Like a fool, I hadn't seen anything coming. Holeraw, Holeraw, of course it was... it was WARHOLE! Was the nightmare really starting again?!

SORRY, BUT YES. THE NIGHTMARE IS STARTING AGAIN.

NIKE !

PAMELA !

NIKE...

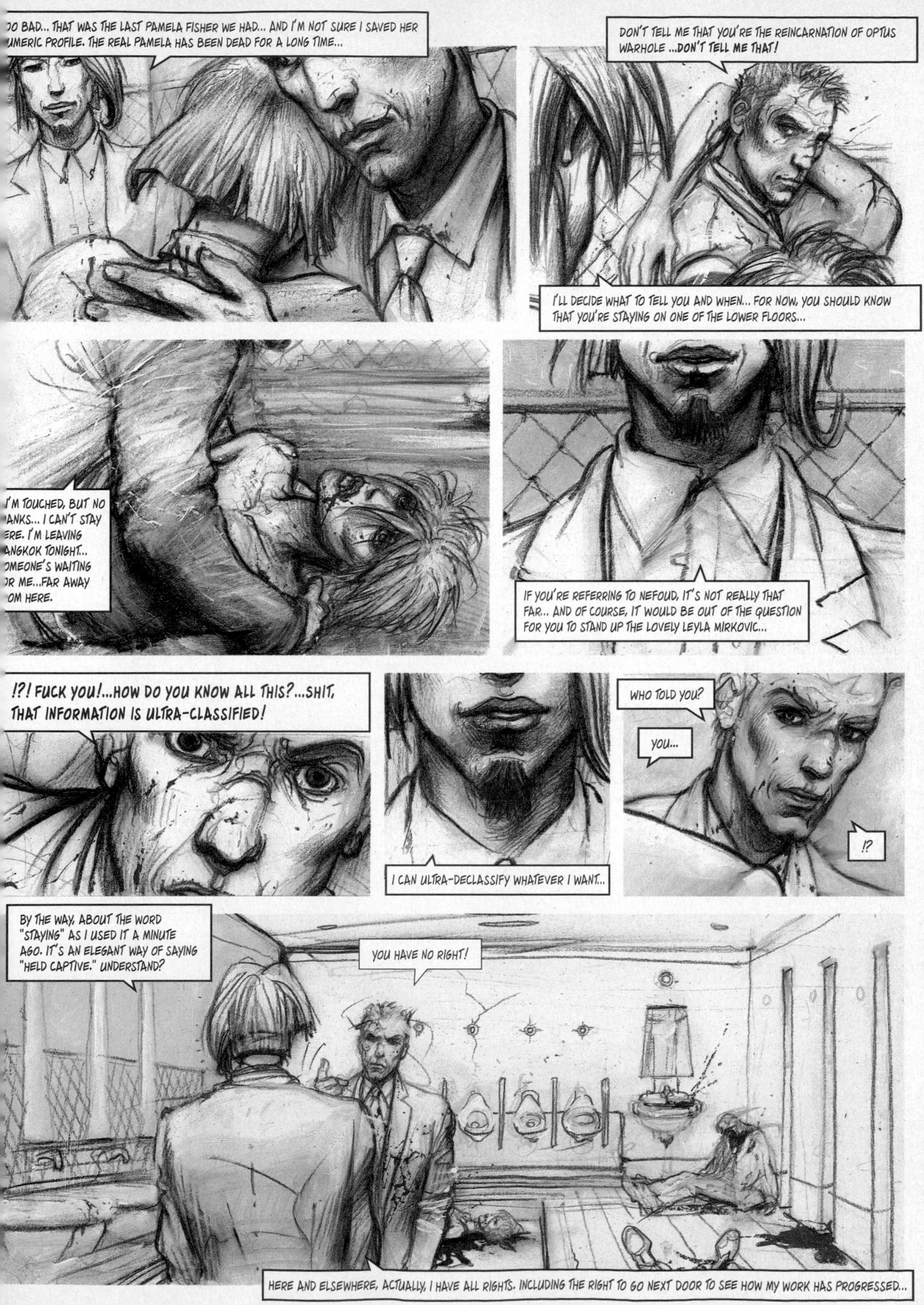
OO BAD... THAT WAS THE LAST PAMELA FISHER WE HAD... AND I'M NOT SURE I SAVED HER UMERIC PROFILE. THE REAL PAMELA HAS BEEN DEAD FOR A LONG TIME...
DON'T TELL ME THAT YOU'RE THE REINCARNATION OF OPTUS WARHOLE ...DON'T TELL ME THAT!
I'LL DECIDE WHAT TO TELL YOU AND WHEN... FOR NOW, YOU SHOULD KNOW THAT YOU'RE STAYING ON ONE OF THE LOWER FLOORS...
I'M TOUCHED, BUT NO ANKS... I CAN'T STAY ERE. I'M LEAVING ANGKOK TONIGHT... OMEONE'S WAITING OR ME...FAR AWAY OM HERE.
IF YOU'RE REFERRING TO NEFOUD, IT'S NOT REALLY THAT FAR... AND OF COURSE, IT WOULD BE OUT OF THE QUESTION FOR YOU TO STAND UP THE LOVELY LEYLA MIRKOVIC...
!?! FUCK YOU!...HOW DO YOU KNOW ALL THIS?...SHIT, THAT INFORMATION IS ULTRA-CLASSIFIED!
I CAN ULTRA-DECLASSIFY WHATEVER I WANT...
WHO TOLD YOU?
YOU...
!?
BY THE WAY, ABOUT THE WORD "STAYING" AS I USED IT A MINUTE AGO. IT'S AN ELEGANT WAY OF SAYING "HELD CAPTIVE." UNDERSTAND?
YOU HAVE NO RIGHT!
HERE AND ELSEWHERE, ACTUALLY, I HAVE ALL RIGHTS. INCLUDING THE RIGHT TO GO NEXT DOOR TO SEE HOW MY WORK HAS PROGRESSED...

...A WORK THAT, IF I REMEMBER CORRECTLY, YOU BEGAN WITH THE MAGICAL FIRST BRUSHSTROKE, MY DEAR NIKE HATZFELD.

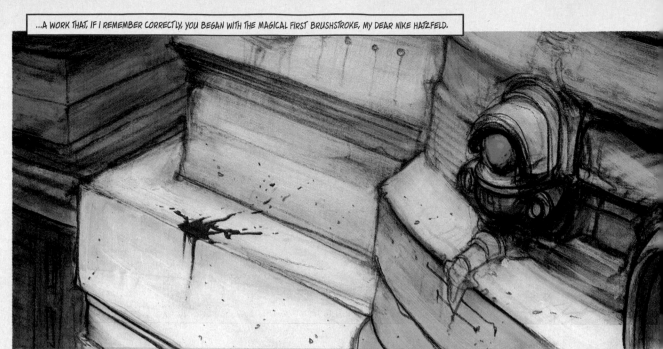

AT THAT SAME MOMENT, ON BOARD AN EAST ASIAN AIRLINES PLANE, DESTINATION AMMAN, PORT OF NEFOUD...

IF I MAY, MR. HATZFELD. YOU'LL BE MORE COMFORTABLE WITH YOUR SEAT BACK.

...AND ON THE CHINA EXPRESS, DESTINATION IRKOUTSK.

HATZFELD? WHAT KIND OF NAME IS THAT?

So, I'm being held captive. So, I missed my specially coded flight to Nefoud. The flight for Leyla. And there's no way to warn her. And there's no way to escape the doubt.

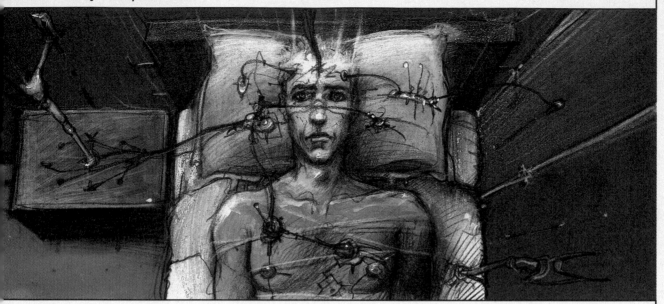

Because doubting that you're made of real flesh and real blood gives you a dizzy feeling, even when you're lying down. It's amplified by a permanent state of panic, the least significant effect of which is the total inability to sleep.
After obsessively feeling every part of my body, after "listening" to what could be "heard," after trying to analyze every tiny secretion, every odor, I arrived at the reasonable conclusion that I was human and that I was, therefore, the real Nike Hatzfeld. But the memory of the taste of Pamela's perfectly imitated blood would plunge me back into the abyss of doubt, sweeping away all certainty of, say, my urine, or my saliva, or my ever present sweat's authenticity. But who can say that the artistic carnage of the anagrammed pseudo-Warhole, of Milorad Zivkovic thrown into the void from the sixty-seventh floor, of this cell where I'm being held in a tower in Bangkok, who can say that all of this is not just a manifestation of a state peculiar to human beings, a state called: "a nightmare"?
That's it. I'm in the clutches of an organized nightmare, which you could call: "paranoia."

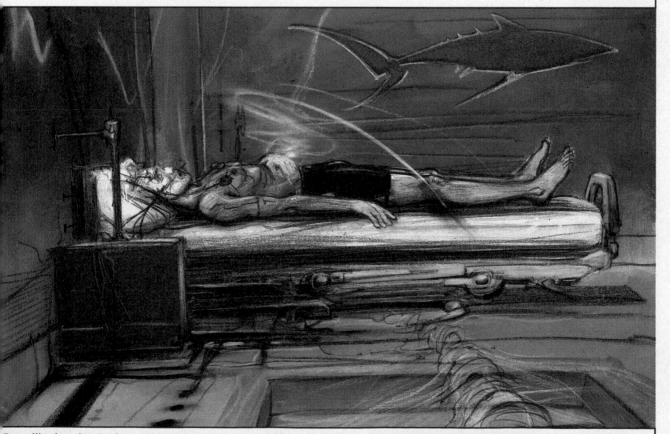

But still, why, when I rub myself just above my pubis and higher, don't I hear the reassuring gurgling of a few good meters of intestine? Where are my intestines? Do I even have any?

AMIR

"You have suffered a partial mutation effect from a chemically contaminated fly, one of the innumerable varieties conceived by the sadly famous Optus Warhole... I will do everything I can to isolate the mutation. I can assure you that the effect is only superficial and will only affect your pigmentation. I'm already working on the antidote."
This was the general diagnosis of Rinat Gazzaev, the imperturbable scientific researcher and moderate Muslim, as I managed, with my last drop of carburant, to reach a new "entryway."

THERE ARE A LOT OF PEOPLE UP THERE.

IT'S STRANGE, NO ONE EVER COMES HERE. THIS PORT WAS TURNED INTO AN ORTHODOX TOMB FOR THE SINO-RUSSO-MONGOL CONFLICT... TWO MILLION DEAD.

WHAT DOES IT MEAN? SHOULD WE TURN AROUND?

WE'LL FILL UP AND WAIT UNTIL TOMORROW. THE WEATHER'S TOO BAD FOR US TO GO ANY FURTHER EAST.

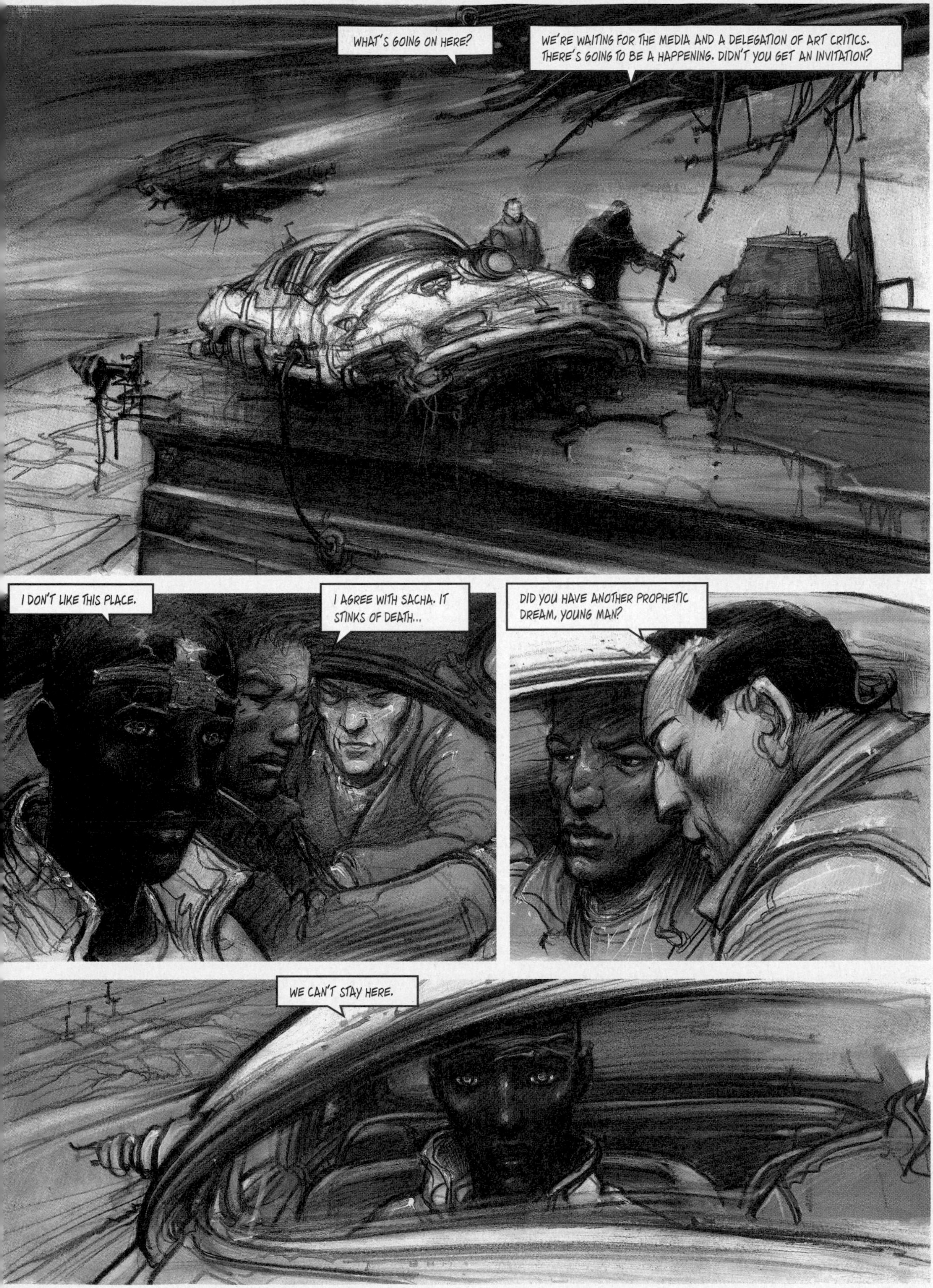
WHAT'S GOING ON HERE?
WE'RE WAITING FOR THE MEDIA AND A DELEGATION OF ART CRITICS. THERE'S GOING TO BE A HAPPENING. DIDN'T YOU GET AN INVITATION?
I DON'T LIKE THIS PLACE.
I AGREE WITH SACHA. IT STINKS OF DEATH...
DID YOU HAVE ANOTHER PROPHETIC DREAM, YOUNG MAN?
WE CAN'T STAY HERE.

He came after Hector Jolibois, the brand new President of the World Political and Economic Confederation, Judith Clayborne, President of the New United Nations, Xhiu Tom Tum, Emperor of the New Autonomous Asian Territory, Simone Wizmann and Jeremy Upshaw, 2026 Nobel prize winners in medicine and astrophysics respectively, the Ayatollah Kharsella, the Dalaï Lama, the Great Rabbi Yazhavy and Pope Paul IX. And after them, Nike was, like I said, the tenth and final witness to the Eagle Site. I was taking wicked pleasure in giving him the news bit by bit and then watching his excitement turn sour.

98

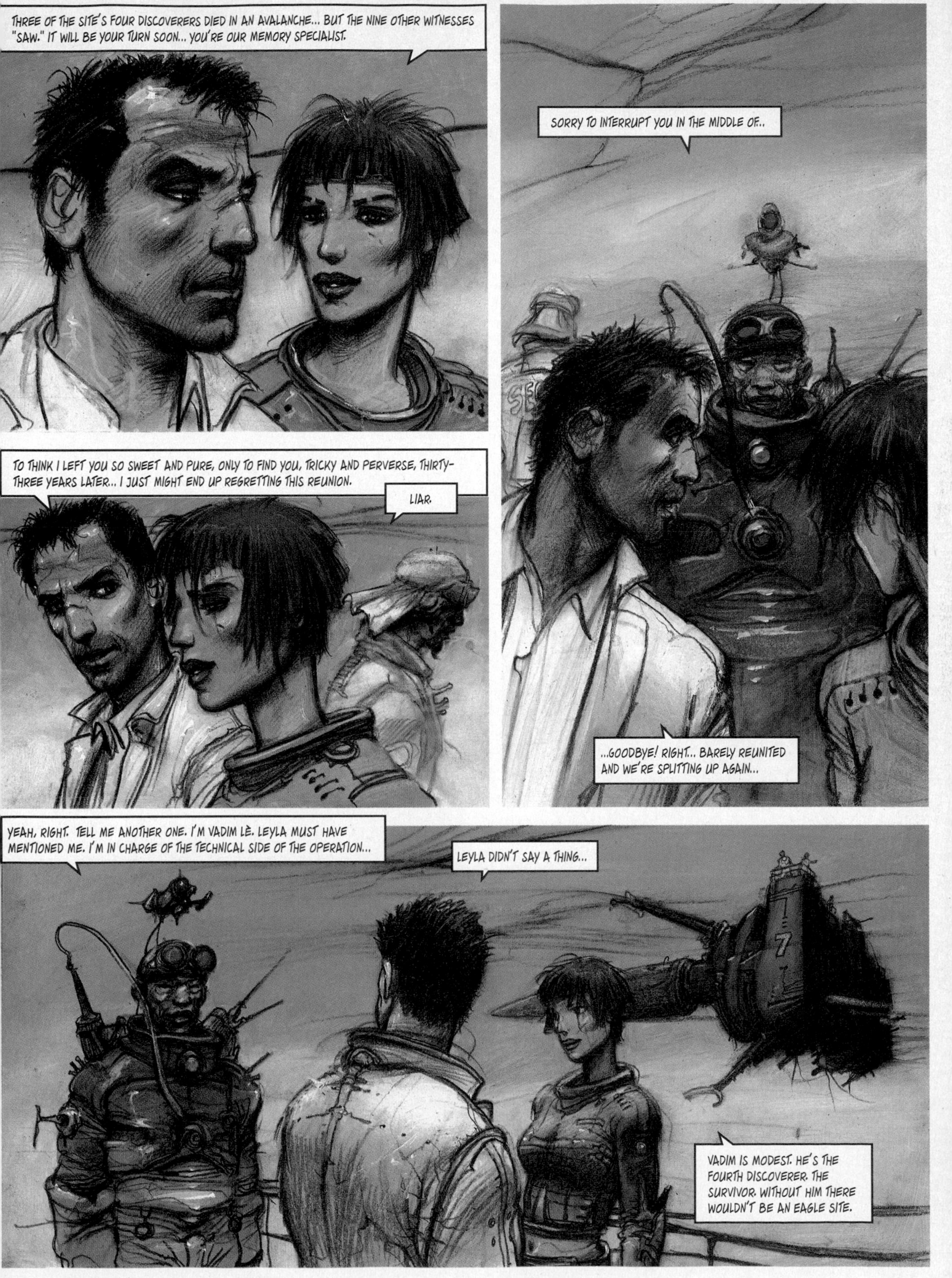
THREE OF THE SITE'S FOUR DISCOVERERS DIED IN AN AVALANCHE... BUT THE NINE OTHER WITNESSES "SAW." IT WILL BE YOUR TURN SOON... YOU'RE OUR MEMORY SPECIALIST.
SORRY TO INTERRUPT YOU IN THE MIDDLE OF..
TO THINK I LEFT YOU SO SWEET AND PURE, ONLY TO FIND YOU, TRICKY AND PERVERSE, THIRTY-THREE YEARS LATER... I JUST MIGHT END UP REGRETTING THIS REUNION.
LIAR.
...GOODBYE! RIGHT... BARELY REUNITED AND WE'RE SPLITTING UP AGAIN...
YEAH, RIGHT. TELL ME ANOTHER ONE. I'M VADIM LÈ. LEYLA MUST HAVE MENTIONED ME. I'M IN CHARGE OF THE TECHNICAL SIDE OF THE OPERATION...
LEYLA DIDN'T SAY A THING...
VADIM IS MODEST. HE'S THE FOURTH DISCOVERER. THE SURVIVOR. WITHOUT HIM THERE WOULDN'T BE AN EAGLE SITE.

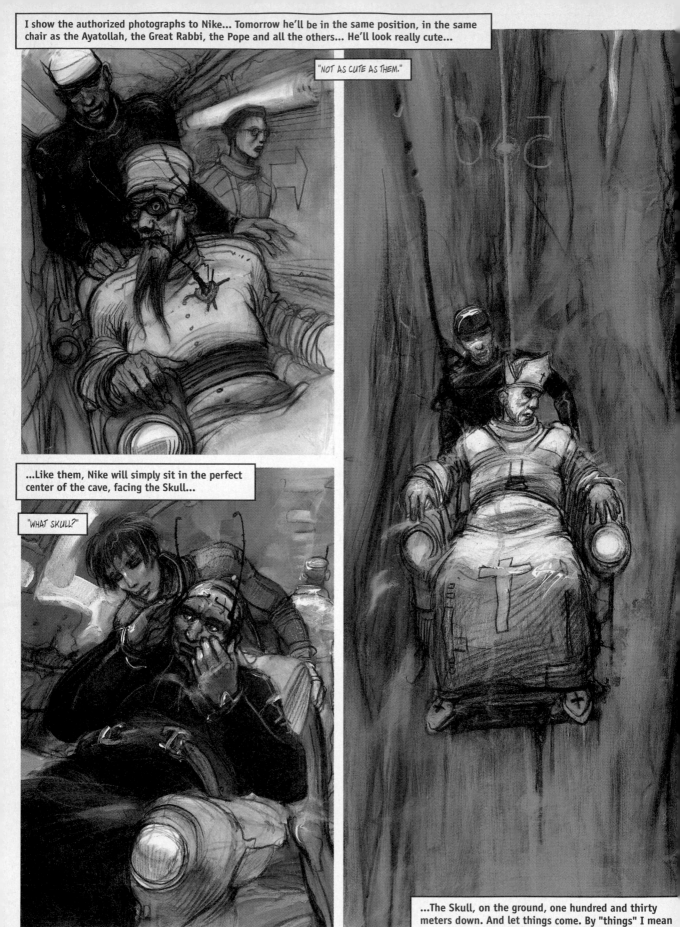

I show the authorized photographs to Nike... Tomorrow he'll be in the same position, in the same chair as the Ayatollah, the Great Rabbi, the Pope and all the others... He'll look really cute...

"NOT AS CUTE AS THEM."

...Like them, Nike will simply sit in the perfect center of the cave, facing the Skull...

"WHAT SKULL?"

...The Skull, on the ground, one hundred and thirty meters down. And let things come. By "things" I mean the waves of information, a kind of message.

..Like the nine before him, he'll have to record the experience as accurately as possible. And then he will give everything to the on-site guards, who are also under oath.

...AND THEN? I GUESS YOU COMPARE ALL OF THE MESSAGES...

EXACTLY. AND WE MATCH THEM UP WITH THE EVIDENCE THAT VADIM GATHERED JUST BEFORE THE SECOND GALLERY CRUMBLED.

I'm happy to be sharing this adventure with Nike and to have him all to myself tonight.

WHAT YOU'RE ABOUT TO SEE IS ALL THAT REMAINS OF HIS ORIGINAL BODY. BUT IT'S OBVIOUSLY THE MOST PRECIOUS PART. WE ARE FORTY METERS BELOW THE BUILDING AND YOU ARE VERY FORTUNATE TO GAIN ACCESS. IT IS THE VIRTUAL HEART OF HIS MIND.

THERE ARE SOME PRIVILEGES I WOULDN'T MIND SACRIFICING.

To be honest, the original head of Optus Warhole was an obscene sight.

THE BRAIN IS PERFECTLY INTACT. IT'S ACTUALLY BEEN OPTIMIZED BY SEVERAL BORROWINGS FROM OTHER GRAY MATTER. FIRST WE TOOK THE MEMORY FROM YOURS, THANKS TO PAMELA'S FIRST NUMERICAL REPLICA. THEN WE BORROWED FROM SEVERAL OF THE "GUESTS" AT THE ALL WHITE HAPPENING... BRILLIANT AND HIGHLY SPECIALIZED PEOPLE FOR THE MOST PART...

Nothing's lost on that Warhole vulture, I thought

102

SOME PARTS OF THE BODY WERE GRAFTED ONTO OLDER MODELS, OTHERS COULDN'T BE SAVED. BUT THE GOAL WAS ULTIMATELY TO CREATE A MODEL THAT WOULD BE PERFECT IN EVERY WAY.

THE BRAIN CONCEIVED OF THIS MODEL. IT IS STANDING IN FRONT OF YOU.

U'RE THE PERFECTION?

M THE PERFECTION.

YOU MIGHT NOT AGREE, MR. HATZFELD, BUT MINE IS THE FORM I DREAMED OF NATURE DIDN'T SPOIL ME WHEN I WAS "ALIVE," YOU SEE... THE WAY I LOOK TODAY, BELIEVE ME, I WREAK HAVOC AMONG BOTH WOMEN AND MEN...

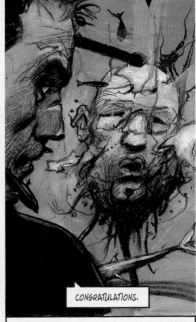

CONGRATULATIONS.

The head's voice was as obscene as the head itself. Combined...

YOUR PRIVATE COMMENTS ARE LESS THAN FLATTERING, MR. HATZFELD.

THEN I'LL STOP THINKING.

ONLY AFTER YOU LISTEN TO WHAT I HAVE TO SAY. IF YOU DON'T MIND.
FIRST OF ALL, I'D LIKE TO REASSURE YOU THAT YOU ARE THE REAL NIKE HATZFELD.

WHEW...

SECONDLY, TWO OF YOUR REPLICAS ARE OUT IN THE WORLD RIGHT NOW. ONE AT THE EAGLE SITE IN THE NEFOUD DESERT AND THE OTHER IN IRKOUTSK IN EXTREME ORIENTAL SIBERIA. THESE TWO REPLICAS ARE NOT AWARE THAT THEY ARE COPIES. THEY ARE PRO-GRAMMED TO BELIEVE THAT THEY ARE EACH THE UNIQUE NIKE HATZFELD. IN OTHER WORDS, EACH IS IGNORANT OF THE OTHER'S EXISTENCE AS WELL AS OF YOURS.

I'M NOT SURE I LIKE THIS STORY.

THIRD AND LASTLY — AND THIS IS THE POINT OF THE EXPERIMENT — YOU SHOULD BE ABLE TO FOLLOW, OR, IN A SENSE, TO "LIVE" THE LIVES OF YOUR TWO REPLICAS. YOU'LL WEAR A SPECIAL HELMET FOR THESE... "INCURSIONS." I WILL BE PERMANENTLY PLUGGED INTO YOUR "VISIONS," BUT YOU WILL BE FREE TO REMOVE THE HELMET IF YOU FEEL THE NEED TO DO SO. WHAT TAKES PLACE MAY PROVE TO BE QUITE TRYING. YOUR TWO REPLICAS ARE IN POSSESSION OF YOUR ENTIRE MEMORY, ALL OF YOUR PHYSICAL AND MENTAL TRAITS, YOUR WHOLE "STORY," IF YOU LIKE. THE ONLY DIFFERENCE IS THAT THE IRKOUTSK REPLICA, FOR CERTAIN "SCRIPTING" REASONS, IS UNAWARE OF LEYLA MIRKOVIC'S CALL FROM NEFOUD AND OF THE HOLERAW INVITATION, WHICH YOU SO OBLIGINGLY ACCEPTED AND TO WHICH WE OWE THE PLEASURE OF THIS EXCITING... TÊTE À TÊTE...

IT'S ONLY EXCITING TO YOU.

PERHAPS. BUT I'M GROWING IMPATIENT...
THE HELMET IS WAITING. IT IS TIME FOR YOU TO LEARN THE PROCESS. I HAVE IMPORTANT THINGS TO SEE WITH YOUR EYES... GESTATING HAPPENINGS, EXPERIMENTS...

WELL THEN?... WHICH LIFE WILL YOU STEP INTO?
THAT OF THE HATZFELD IN THE SIBERIAN COLD,
OR THE HATZFELD IN THE SAUDI DESERT?
I'D SUGGEST BOTH AT ONCE.

AND I SUGGEST THAT YOU LEAVE ME RIGHT HERE WITH THE REAL NIKE HATZFELD'S LIFE... MINE, ME ALONE AND WITHOUT THE FISH, PLEASE!

WHAT FISH?

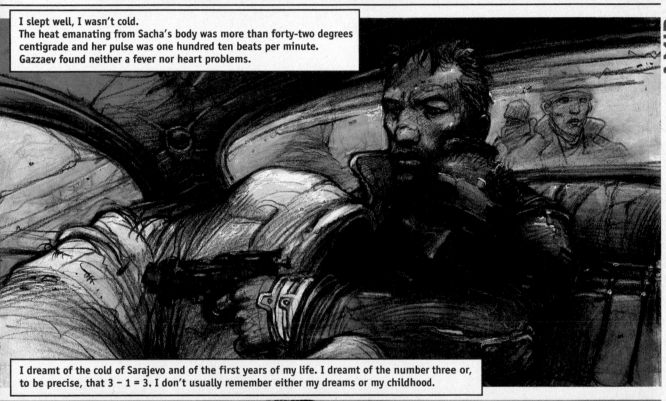

I slept well, I wasn't cold.
The heat emanating from Sacha's body was more than forty-two degrees centigrade and her pulse was one hundred ten beats per minute. Gazzaev found neither a fever nor heart problems.

I dreamt of the cold of Sarajevo and of the first years of my life. I dreamt of the number three or, to be precise, that $3 - 1 = 3$. I don't usually remember either my dreams or my childhood.

The delegation of art critics took their places in the official gallery. Gazzaev, who wasn't especially crazy about art, said he was excited about this happening. I had a horrible feeling about it. I decided to stay close to Sacha.

First, there was a muffled groaning sound, not thunder or anything else I could identify. Then a vile odor filled the cold air, an exhalation from the mouth of the grave.

Black liquid dripped onto their faces.

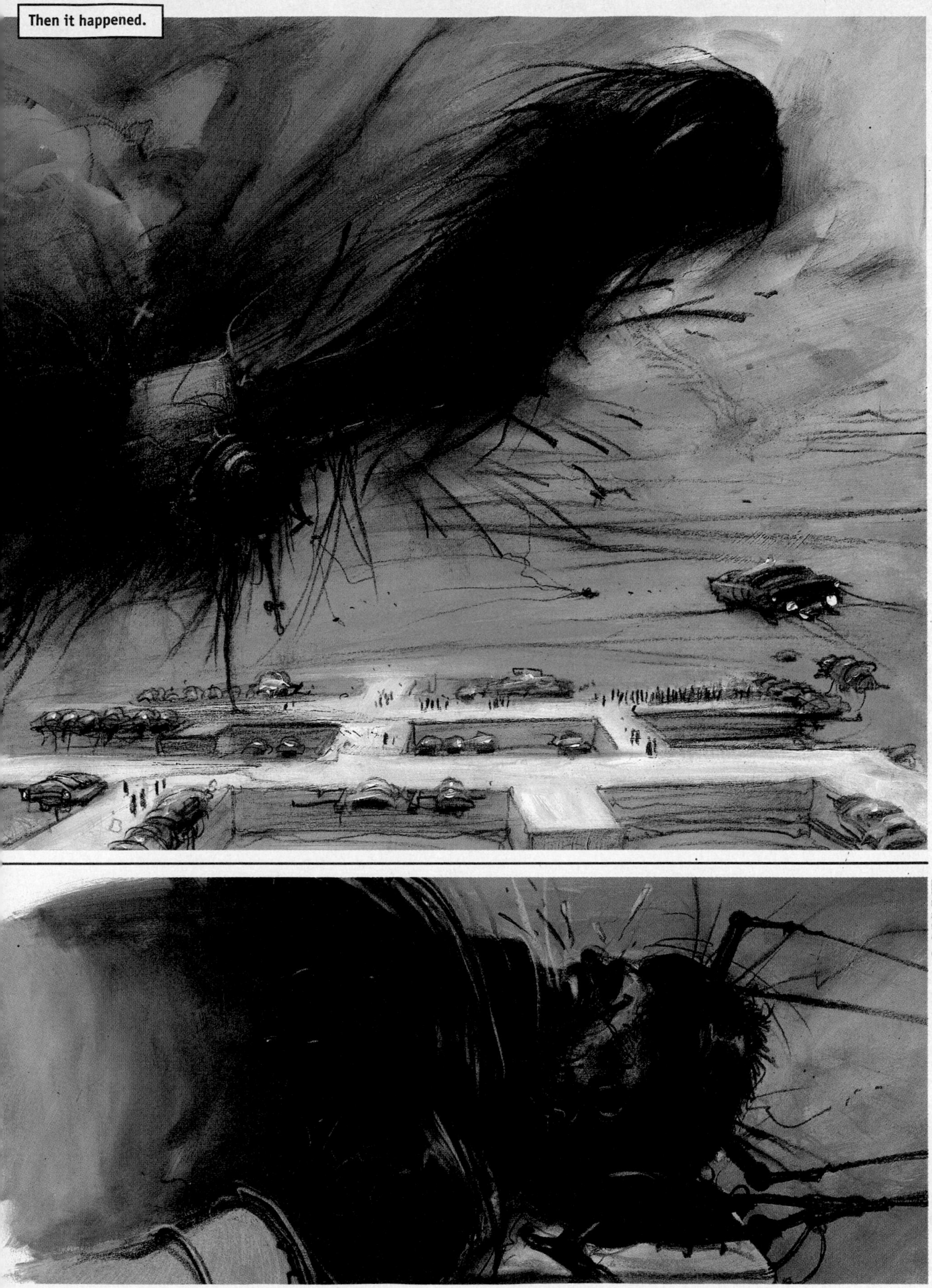
Then it happened.

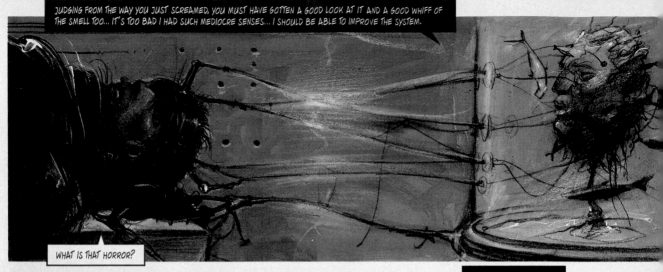

JUDGING FROM THE WAY YOU JUST SCREAMED, YOU MUST HAVE GOTTEN A GOOD LOOK AT IT AND A GOOD WHIFF OF THE SMELL TOO... IT'S TOO BAD I HAD SUCH MEDIOCRE SENSES... I SHOULD BE ABLE TO IMPROVE THE SYSTEM.

WHAT IS THAT HORROR?

ERUPTED DEATH COMPRESSION. MY MOST RECENT WORK... YOU DON'T LIKE IT?

IT WILL PROPAGATE IN THE FORM OF A COMPACT CLOUD, MOVING AT THE MERCY OF THE WINDS, OR ACCORDING TO MY WILL. BEFORE DISINTEGRATING, IT WILL EMIT RAINS COMPOSED OF TEARS ISSUED FROM THE DECOMPOSITION OF TWO MILLION SOLDIERS AND CIVILIANS DEAD ON THE FIELD OF FOOLISHNESS...

IT IS A UNIVERSAL WORK. AGAINST WAR AND THE BLINDING OF MANKIND. BUT THERE WILL BE A PRICE TO PAY. A KIND OF BOOMERANG EFFECT.

IT'S NOT ART BRUT, IT'S BRUTAL ART.

AMIR

Dozens of bodies writhed in pain. The delegation of critics seemed to have the worst time of it. The drops of black rain bored holes in everything they touched and I'm sure there were deaths.

I didn't see Gazzaev, but I chose to stay close to Sacha, who was still sleeping, rather than go look for him.

The vile cloud's mass seemed to grow as it moved away. I guessed that it was already more than two hundred and fifty meters across...

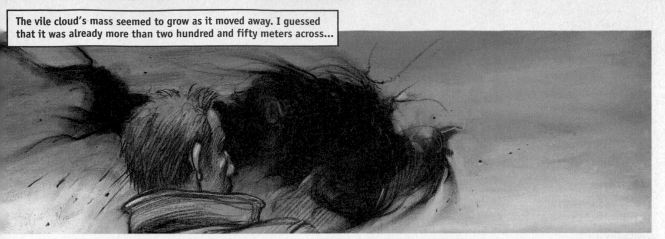

DO YOU KNOW THE ARTIST'S NAME?

NO. I'M JUST HERE BY CHANCE. I WASN'T INVITED.

IF OPTUS WARHOLE HAD GONE INTO CONCEPTUAL ART HE COULDN'T HAVE DONE A BETTER JOB.

WARHOLE IS DEAD.

HOW DO YOU KNOW?

HE'S DEAD. I WAS THERE.

YOU WERE THERE? DO YOU KNOW THAT THE FRIENDS OF MY ENEMIES ARE MY ENEMIES?

WARHOLE WASN'T A FRIEND.

IN THAT CASE, LET ME INTRODUCE MYSELF: NIKE HATZFELD.

AMIR FAZLAGIC.

NIKE

THIS IS INSANE. YOUR GODDAMN REPLICA OF ME REALLY BELIEVES THAT HE'S ME!!!

IT'S QUITE A SUCCESS, IF I DO SAY SO MYSELF.. BUT YOU CAN GO ON TO NEFOUD IF YOU NEED A LITTLE BREAK...

NO WAY! I'M NOT PLAYING ANYMORE.

GO ON TO NEFOUD. THAT'S AN ORDER.

LEYLA

Nike told me the good news and the night was even more beautiful than before. Amir is alive. We will find him just as soon as the Eagle Site "releases" us.

"When?" Nike asked impatiently.

ONE DAY IN DECEMBER. A DAY THAT YOU WON'T BE ABLE TO KEEP FROM TALKING ABOUT SOON, AFTER THE SKULL EXPERIMENT...

NIKE

FUCKING BASTARD!

DID YOU SEE SOMETHING THAT UPSET YOU?

HE'S GOT HIS HANDS ALL OVER HER!

AND IT SEEMS YOU DIDN'T FEEL ANYTHING AT ALL... HOW INFURIATING... I'LL TRY TO IMPROVE THAT TOO...

AND BESIDES, HE'S GOT A TAN! THE JERK'S GOT A TAN!

SLIGHT PROBLEM WITH THE COLOR METER. IT HAPPENS...

FUCK YOU, WARHOLE! WHAT DO YOU WANT FROM ME? WHAT'S THE POINT OF ALL THIS?

I HAVE EIGHTEEN HOLERAW REPLICAS WAITING FOR THE GREENLIGHT. YOU'RE HERE FOR THE FINAL TEST. IF THE EXPERIMENT WITH YOUR TWO REPLICAS IS CONCLUSIVE, THEN I WILL BEGIN MY OPERATION. JUST IMAGINE, BEING IN EIGHTEEN PLACES IN THE WORLD AT ONCE, IN KEY SPOTS, CREATING A NETWORK THAT COULD ALL BE CONTROLLED FROM HERE... CAN YOU IMAGINE?

YES, PERFECTLY... YOU WANT MORE POWER. THAT'S NOTHING NEW...

AND THE PLEASURE OF CREATION, THE A.E.A., WHAT DO YOU THINK OF THAT?

THE A.E. WHAT?

ABSOLUTE EVIL ART.

THE ART OF SUPREME EVIL... I THINK YOU GOT A LITTLE TASTE OF IT AT MY PARTY AND YOU EVEN MADE A CONTRIBUTION YOURSELF. IMAGINE THE SAME THING ON A GRANDER SCALE... THE SCALE OF BUSINESSES, CULTS, RELIGIONS, NATIONS, RACES...

AND WHY NOT GENES, CELLS, BACTERIA, VIRUSES... OR HOW ABOUT ORPHANS WHO HAVEN'T SEEN EACH OTHER FOR THIRTY-THREE YEARS...

...OR ALL OF IT AT ONCE...

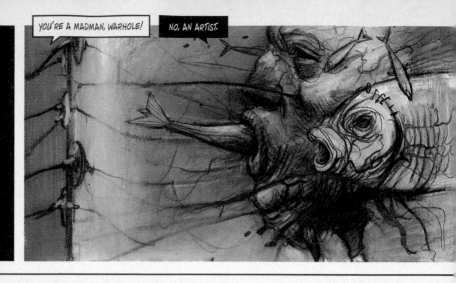

AMIR

Gazzaev died in Sacha's arms, a hole bored in his skull by a drop of black rain. "I'm sorry about the antidote, dear. I'm sorry," were his last words. "I'm fine like this," Sacha answered, just a fraction of a second too late.

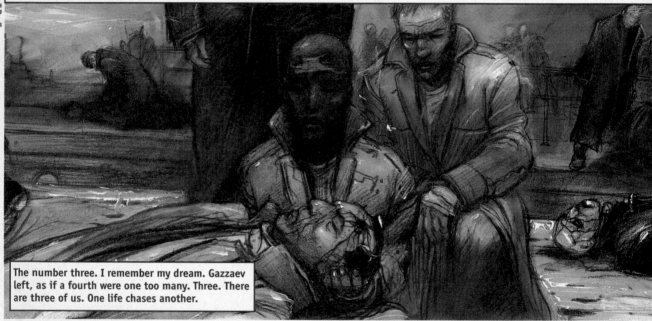

The number three. I remember my dream. Gazzaev left, as if a fourth were one too many. Three. There are three of us. One life chases another.

Nike told me about Sarajevo and our three-part story: him, Leyla and me. Why does everything always happen in threes? When we find Leyla, there will be four of us. Which life will be the one too many then? The idea that it could be Sacha's is utterly unbearable to me.

Nike, whose existence I'd been unaware of just a few hours earlier, took things brutally in hand, with a christlike attitude that Sacha, who had retreated into herself, seemed to dislike.

My "savior" (that's what he called himself) had an idea: to win back Irkoutsk and to gain access to obscure research networks in an attempt to locate Leyla and what he called "the Eagle Site."

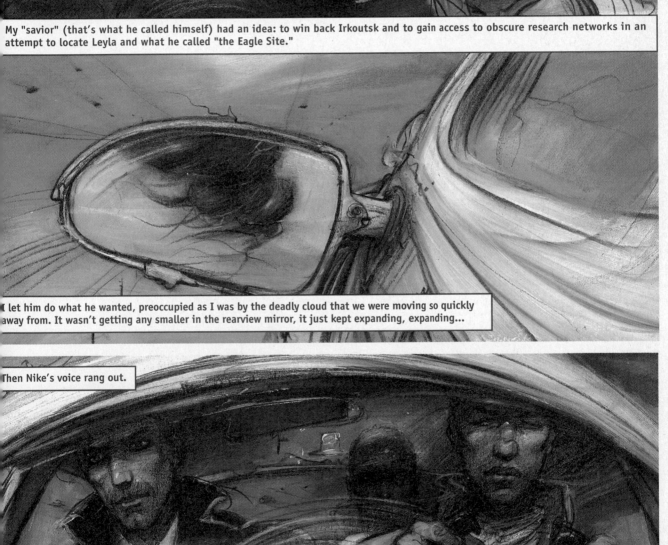

I let him do what he wanted, preoccupied as I was by the deadly cloud that we were moving so quickly away from. It wasn't getting any smaller in the rearview mirror, it just kept expanding, expanding...

Then Nike's voice rang out.

SNIPERS ARE ALL ASSHOLES.

LET'S GO TO NEFOUD, NOW!

My brain spun around on itself, standing at attention to the Very Great Artist whose head was marinating in its jar. I made contact with my replica in Nefoud, but then, in the same fraction of a second, lost consciousness.

DO YOU KNOW WHY THEY'RE ALL ASSHOLES, AMIR?

There was a synthetic bitterness in Nike's voice.

BECAUSE YOUR FATHER WAS ONE OF THEM... AN ASSHOLE SNIPER...

Just don't answer.

A BITCH OF A SNIPER WHO KILLED MY FATHER AND ALMOST KILLED ME WITH THE SAME BULLET.

HOW DOES IT FEEL TO BE THE SON OF AN ASSHOLE?

YEAH? HOW DOES THIS FEEL?

The gunshot burst my right eardrum.

114

But I didn't have time to be horrified while my ear was flowing into my throat. Sacha was already explaining. She was unstoppable and sure.

IT WAS ONE OF WARHOLE'S SHITTY, SEMI-SYNTHETIC, POST-OBSCURANTIST CREATURES...A REPLICA. I KNEW IT THE SECOND I TOUCHED IT, WHEN I SHOOK ITS HAND. IT FELT LIKE LIQUID. IT WAS REPULSIVE.

Nike's decapitated corpse bounced indecently on the seat next to me, but Sacha's calm was reassuring, disarming and even healing to my auditory canal.

"So your skin is more sensitive now?" I asked foolishly, missing the whole point.

YOU GOT IT, AMIR. MY SKIN IS MORE SENSITIVE, IT'S DARKER AND YOU LIKE IT EVEN BETTER THAN BEFORE... YOU AND I WILL BE BACK ON TOP AGAIN SOON.

On top again, together again... For that and for everything else, Sacha deserved a kiss.

Nike stayed in the cave as long as the nine others had.

Like the nine others, as soon as he came out he asked the guard for a piece of paper and a pencil and, like the nine others, he was silent for many hours.

At last, like the nine others, his first sentence was a triple question, the same as the others, word for word: "What does carbon 14 and a half tell about the bones and the shell? What does a comparison with Vadim Lé's report tell us about the buried cave? When is December 32nd?"

I regained consciousness but it was a shaky consciousness, semi-paralyzed and black and blue. Soon enough, I felt Warhole rushing in. He said: "We hit a little snag with the Irkoutsk replica..."

...BUT WE'LL GET OUR HANDS ON THAT MUTANT-SKINNED EX-ERADICATOR KRYLOVA ONE OF THESE DAYS...

FORTUNATELY, THE NEFOUD REPLICA WAS MARVELOUS. THE IMAGES WE IMPORTED ARE OF A UNIQUE AND UNEQUALLED ARTISTIC VALUE... A MONUMENT TO THE UNIVERSAL ABSOLUTE!

"IS THAT THE VERY GREAT ARTIST OF SUPREME EVIL SPEAKING? YOUR HUMILITY IS OVERWHELMING."

I WEPT WHEN I SAW THOSE IMAGES, MR. HATZFELD. BELIEVE IT OR NOT, I WEPT.

YOU CAN WEEP INSIDE OF A JAR FULL OF LIQUID?

IT COULD CAUSE AN OVERFLOW, BUT I APPRECIATE YOUR HUMOR, NIKE.

OH, SO WE'RE FRIENDS NOW? WATCH OUT, THAT KIND OF SLIP OF THE TONGUE IN WHAT'S LEFT OF YOUR MOUTH, THAT'S CALLED A "REVOLUTION..."

"Precisely. The time has come to tell the world about my revolutionary discovery," he said as his holy perfection unplugged me.

WARHOLE, DISCOVERER OF THE EAGLE SITE?

Seventy two hours after the media blitz caused by the resurrected monster, Optus Warhole (see also the Arts and Climatology pages), the official Committee of the Eagle Site remains silent.

The cave drawing (below), widely distributed by certain sources of information, illicit or otherwise, is evidence either of the kind of fantastical hoax of which Warhole is perfectly capable, or of the most complete and fundamental questioning of the knowledge we have until now amassed on the origins of humanity and the universe. The ten major international witnesses (including Pope Paul IX, the Dalaï Lama, the Ayatollah Kharselleh...) plus the surviving discoverer (who chooses to remain anonymous) who might have concrete proof, are the only ones who could disprove or confirm Warhole's allegations, were they to admit to having lost the race for the discovery, which considering the importance of the event, would be pathetic.

(additional information coded)

WHAT DOES THE CAVE PAINTING SAY?

Drawing attributed by Warhole to one of the ten major witnesses.

Warhole's theory is simple and radical. The humanoid to the right (the artist) is witness to a crime (the giant in the middle is the victim). The dot that the two arrows point to represents a sniper's projectile (Warhole insists upon the term "sniper"). The animal to the left is a tyrannosaurus. Notice that it is "walking" past the giant's legs. According to Warhole, this detail offers a realistic scale of the scene (putting the giant at a height of nearly 30 meters!!!) and would date the scene to the time of dinosaurs (the first cretaceous age, 65 million years ago). Just think of the temporal implications of such a theory.

Does it mean that man was a contemporary of the dinosaurs before the great climactic changes took place? Aberrant, grotesque, all these terms that we use to describe the inconceivable are a part of the riddle. But Warhole insists and "calmly awaits the expert conclusions to the dating of carbon 14 and a half and the identical reports of the ten witnesses of the Eagle Site."

(continued on coded pages)

DEATH CLOUD

Currently raining on Kuala Lumpur.

International scientists and military officials in charge of surrounding the *Erupted Death Compression* phenomenon/work attributed to Optus Warhole are having difficulty devising a unified strategy. At the last count, the death cloud measured more than two kilometers in length and the rate of vile precipitation was increasing.

Remember that standard umbrellas are entirely useless. The number of victims is in the hundreds. It recently rained on a Japanese neo-nuclear plant.

(additional information coded)

GANGRENOUS ART

Joao Mendez-Coe, I.A.C. (Independent Art Critic) attended a murderous happening by Optus Warhole (Erupted Death Compression). There were twelve victims among the spectators and seven among the art critics.
Our critic, who was herself wounded in the face, the right collarbone and both hands, provides us with a pertinent and evolving analysis of Warhole's work, which she considers to be from this point on, one part whole, one part "gangrened" to use his own term.

(subscriber access only)

HOLERAW BUILDING – BANGKOK
67th FLOOR

Warhole

Holographic representation of the three rooms of Optus Warhole's (Holeraw's) *All White Happening*. 87 participants, 61 deaths. Notice that the artist's signature consists of traces of victims' blood.

Click on the bloodstains to see the murders.

NIKE

THE EAGLE SITE REVEALS ITS SECRET

UNBELIEVABLE BUT TRUE

The Eagle Site has made public some of its findings. Speaking on behalf of the ten historic witnesses, Simone Wizmann and Jeremy Upshaw announced several definite conclusions drawn from their work. The following points were touched on.

- The ten drawings, which were created independently by each of the Site's witnesses, are all perfectly identical. It should be noted that the most capable artists (Clayborne, Upshaw, the Dalaï Lama) and the least (The Pope and the Ayatollah Kharselleh, who had never drawn in his life) produced the same results.

- These drawings match the original work in the second cave line for line.

- Photographs taken by the surviving discoverer just before the avalanche have been provided. In addition to the cave painting, they show

The ten historic witnesses display their drawings. In front, from left to right, the artist's bones, fragments of the giant's jaw and the shell.

the artist's skeleton. A femur and a skull fragment were saved by the discoverer (who chooses to remain anonymous).

- The dating of carbon 14 and a half places these bones at 72 million years old. The height of the humanoid was approximately 170 centimeters.

- The pigments taken from the painting's components

(humanoid, dinosaur, giant) all date to the same period as the bones.

- As for the remaining cave, the two principal elements (the oversized skull and the "shell") are still being analyzed. The estimated size of the giant is more than 30 meters. The shell may have created the hole in the skull.

- The last point, for which no explanation is provided, is as

follows: the date of December 32nd was mentioned independently by each of the witnesses.

Warhole's scenario/theory as presented by journalists, though it is now corroborated by these official conclusions, has thus far been received with categorical disbelief.

AMIR

The reflexes we'd had before the Obscurantis Order came back effortlessly, in fewer than forty-eight hours. "The reflexes came looking for us," said Sacha. "They're the ones who need us, not the other way around, just like the parallel steps in Minsk and Lvov are waiting for us and not the other way around." Still, we'll stay out of Moscow. Our tracks are still fresh there.

But one thing had changed. Just one. Before the Obscurantis Order, Sacha was the one who followed me around. Today, I'm the one following her footsteps, her scent, her skin... She's our chief and no one will ever touch a hair on her head again. Whether that hair grows back or not. That's it.

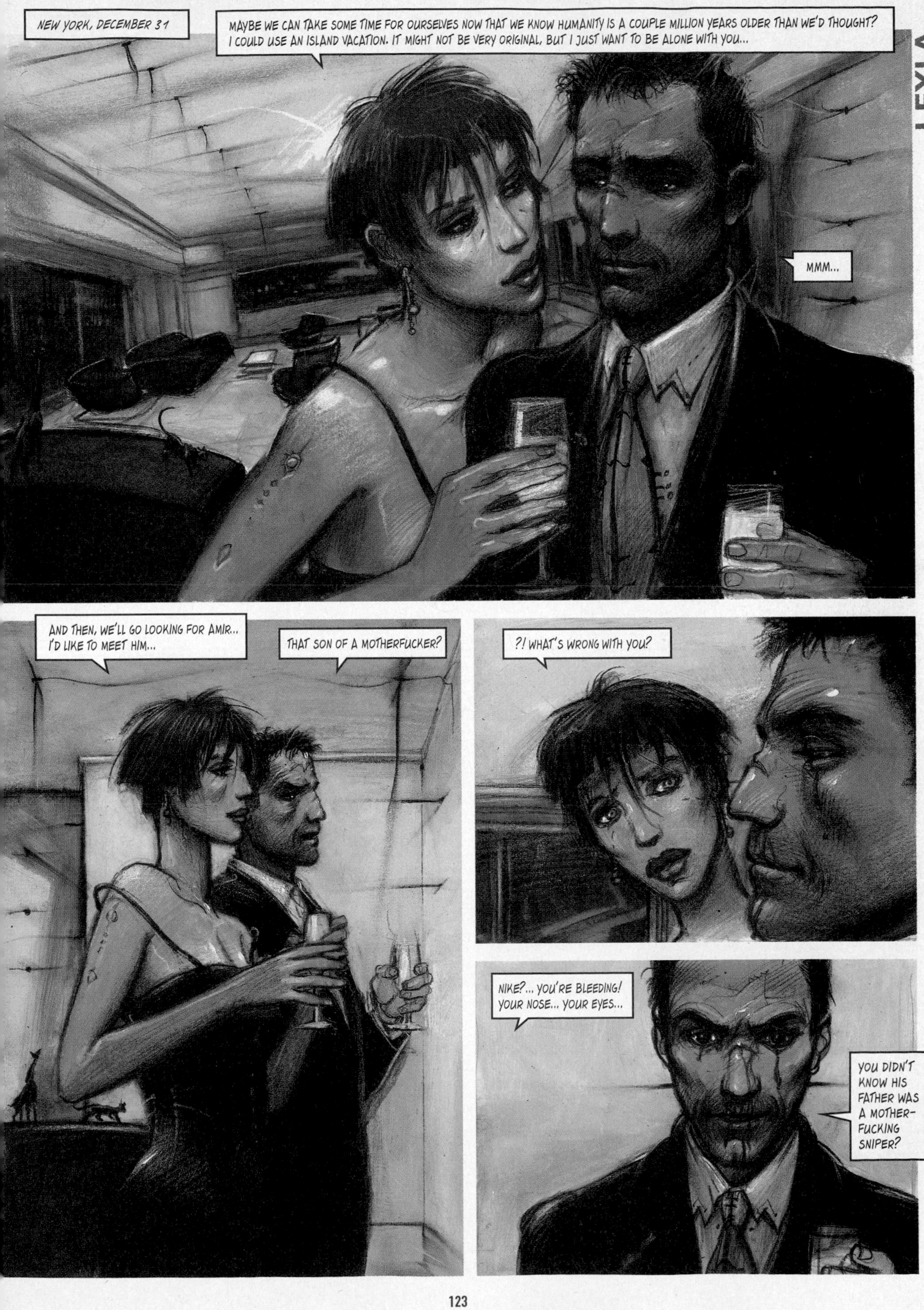
NEW YORK, DECEMBER 31
MAYBE WE CAN TAKE SOME TIME FOR OURSELVES NOW THAT WE KNOW HUMANITY IS A COUPLE MILLION YEARS OLDER THAN WE'D THOUGHT? I COULD USE AN ISLAND VACATION. IT MIGHT NOT BE VERY ORIGINAL, BUT I JUST WANT TO BE ALONE WITH YOU...
MMM...
AND THEN, WE'LL GO LOOKING FOR AMIR... I'D LIKE TO MEET HIM...
THAT SON OF A MOTHERFUCKER?
?! WHAT'S WRONG WITH YOU?
NIKE?... YOU'RE BLEEDING! YOUR NOSE... YOUR EYES...
YOU DIDN'T KNOW HIS FATHER WAS A MOTHER-FUCKING SNIPER?

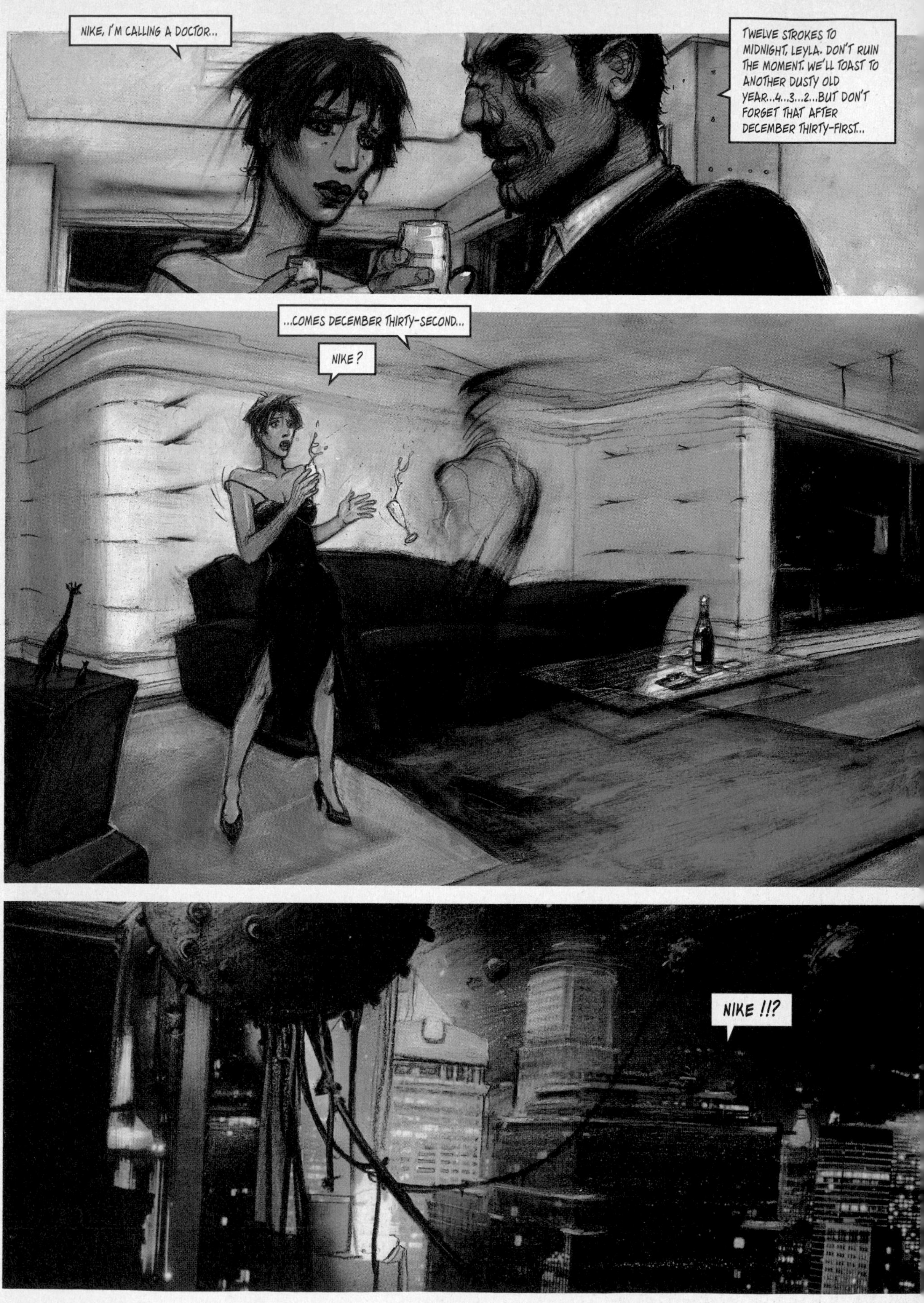
NIKE, I'M CALLING A DOCTOR...
TWELVE STROKES TO MIDNIGHT, LEYLA. DON'T RUIN THE MOMENT. WE'LL TOAST TO ANOTHER DUSTY OLD YEAR...4...3...2...BUT DON'T FORGET THAT AFTER DECEMBER THIRTY-FIRST...
...COMES DECEMBER THIRTY-SECOND...
NIKE ?
NIKE !!?

DAILY NEW YORKER

Friday, January 1, 2027

ALL HAVE VANISHED

Following the incredible discoveries on the Eagle Site, yet another improbable event seems to have occurred. The ten historic observers whose work revolutionized the history of humankind's origins have all physically disappeared in the presence of witnesses. This semi-simultaneous vanishing took place at the twelfth stroke of midnight.

The Ayatollah Karsellah, Pope Paul IX, The Great Rabbi Yazhavy, the Dalaï Lama, Judith Clayborne, Simone Wizmann, Xhiu Tom Tum and Hector Jolibois, all simultaneously vanished during a private reception in Havana. Nike Hatzfeld, who had returned to New York, which is in the same time zone, disappeared at the same moment before the eyes of astrophysicist Leyla Mirkovic. Finally, Jeremy Upshaw, back in Los Angeles (a 3 hour time difference), learning of the disappearance of his friends, decided to be filmed at the fateful moment. At the twelfth stroke of midnight, he disappeared before the lenses of twenty-three cameras.

The witnesses in the three locations confirmed that the last words of the disappeared all made reference to a date: December 32nd.

(information flow continued)

I have never seen Sarajevo in the snow.

LEYLA

The city and the sky form one large piece. I feel integrated into it. I am a part of this still, silent, early morning scene.

As the days go by, Nike's and the other witnesses' disappearance melts further and further into an unpleasant abstraction. Somehow, Nike is outside of my world, he's in another space, an inconceivable space that still produces a void inside of me.

Several times a day, I check for tangible proof of the existence of the Eagle Site but only the sober voice of old Vadim Lé can make me believe, just for a minute, that it was all real. "No one reality looks like another," he says. He's right.

My extremities are frozen and I hardly dare to imagine the reality that haunts me, biting as viciously as Sarajevo's cold.

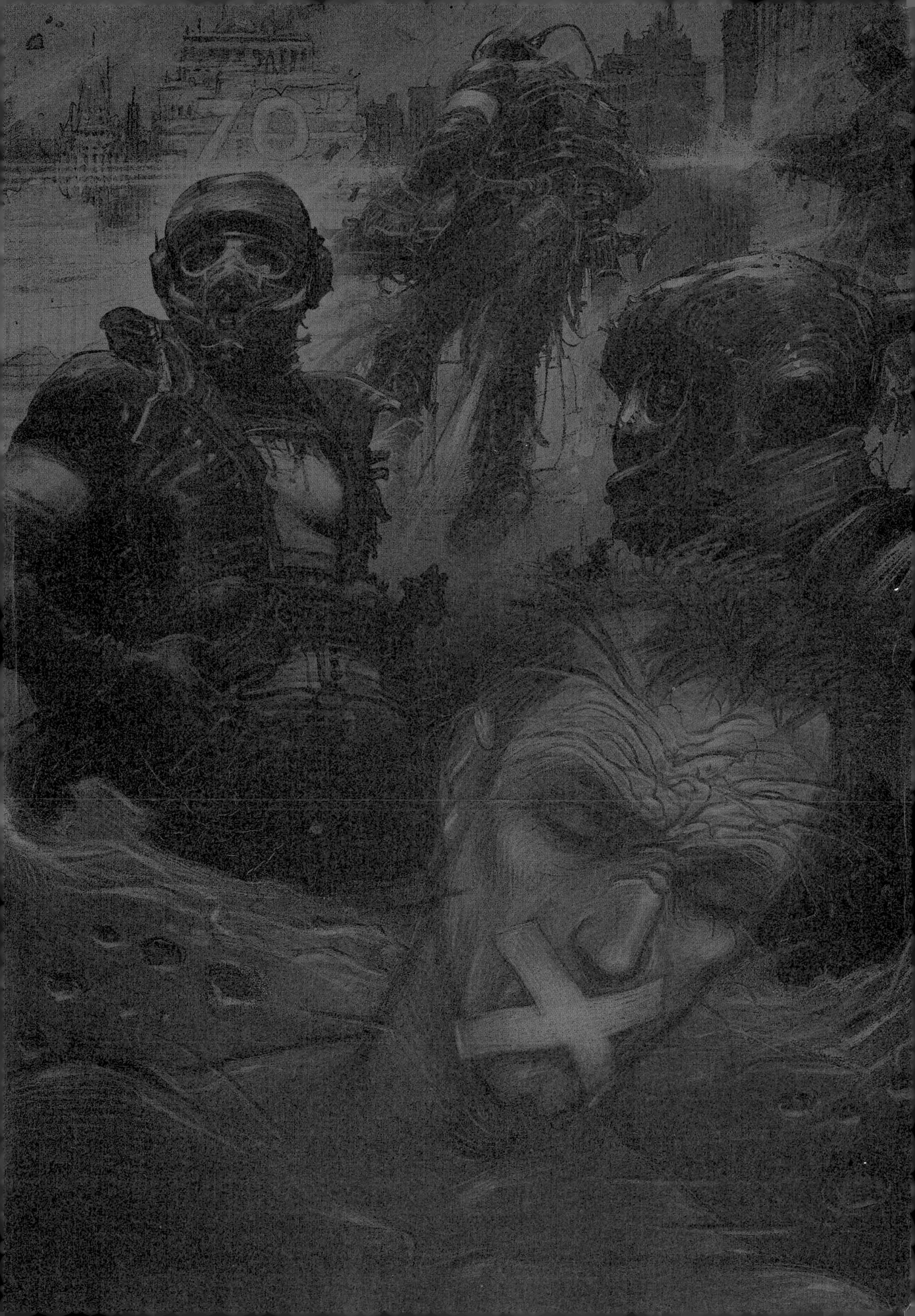

LOOK FOR THESE BOOKS FROM HUMANOIDS/DC COMICS:

THE TECHNOPRIESTS Vol. 1: Initiation
160 pages
Written by Alexandro Jodorowsky
with art by Zoran Janjetov and Fred Beltran

THE HORDE
144 pages
Written and illustrated by Igor Baranko with
colors by Dave Stewart and Charlie Kirchoff

TOWNSCAPES
176 pages
Written by Pierre Christin and illustrated
by Enki Bilal with colors by Dan Brown

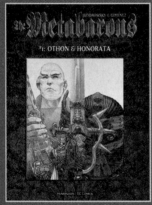

THE METABARONS Vol. 1: Othon & Honorata
136 pages
Written by Alexandro Jodorowsky and
illustrated by Juan Gimenez

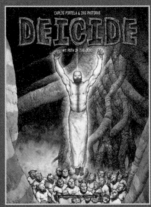

DEICIDE: Vol. 1 PATH OF THE DEAD
112 pages
Written by Carlos Portela and
illustrated by Das Pastoras

THE HOLLOW GROUNDS
192 pages
Written by Luc Schuiten
and illustrated by François Schuiten

THE WHITE LAMA Vol. 1: REINCARNATION
144 pages
Written by Alexandro Jodorowsky
and illustrated by Georges Bess

**CHALAND ANTHOLOGY 1:
FREDDY LOMBARD**
136 pages
By Yves Chaland

To find these books and other titles from Humanoids and DC Comics, call 1-888-comic book
to find the comic shop nearest you, or visit your local bookstore.